ary b ch of
sh.

TACKLERS' TALES

Tacklers' Tales

*An affectionate and humorous collection
of anecdotes, true stories, jokes
… and tacklers' tales*

GEOFFREY MATHER

PALATINE

Tacklers' Tales

Copyright © Geoffrey Mather, 1993, 2003

First published in 1993
by Palatine Books,
an imprint of Carnegie Publishing Ltd
Carnegie Publishing Ltd
Carnegie House,
Chatsworth Road
Lancaster LA1 4SL
www.carnegiepublishing.com

This revised edition published in 2003 by Palatine Books

Reprinted in 2008

British Library Cataloguing-in-Publication data
A catalogue record for this book is available from the British Library

ISBN 978-1-874181-19-4

Cartoons by Ivan Frontani

Typeset by Carnegie Publishing Ltd
Printed and bound by Alden Press, Oxford

CONTENTS

ACKNOWLEDGEMENTS

$\mathcal{M}$OST CONTEMPORARY QUOTATIONS in this book are
the result of my conversations with those concerned.
They include: Thomas Armstrong, Sir John Barbirolli, Helen Bradley,
Charlie Cairoli, Sir Neville Cardus, Violet Carson, Les Dawson, Fred
Dibnah, Dudley Doolittle, Gracie Fields, Mickey Finn, Ray French,
Russell Harty, Thora Hird, Joe Hyman, Albert Modley, Frank Randle,
John Rawnsley, Bill Shankly, Bill Swift, Doris Thomson, Jack Thornley
and Eddie Waring.

A number of newspaper items, including the delightful account of
hysteria in church involving a detachment of the 36th Foot and
Captain Cairns, were collected by Christopher Aspin and form part
of his book *Haslingden 1800–1900* (Haslingden Printing Works, Ltd).
He has also provided additional anecdotes.

A section on clog-making is from a Colne Valley Museum booklet.

Tacklers' tales were contributed from all parts of Lancashire in
response to my newspaper appeal for them. Two entries were from
the unlikely source of Wilton, Connecticut. I acknowledge, with special
thanks, the help of: Mr Norman Bentley, Mr W. Brooks, Mr J. Brooks,
Miss H. Butcher, Mrs M. Courtney, Mrs H. Dalglish, Mr L. Dawson,
Mr J. Dee, Mr G. B. Duff, ARPS, Mrs Meda Edge, Mr J. Fairclough,
Mr C. B. Fawcett, Miss A. Halliwell, Mr A. Hamer, Mr J. C. Hardman,
Mrs Hartley, Mrs E. Iddon, Mr H. Jefferson-Jones (USA), Mr J. King,
Mr D. Lee, Mrs J. McInerney, Mr Barry Riding, Mr J. Rothwell, Mrs
F. Shorrock, Miss W. Slater, Mrs S. Slinger, Mr Derick Stanton,
Mr J. C. Thornber, Mr Roy Wallis, Mr J. Walton, Mr Harry Westwell,
Mr T. Whitaker, Mr W. Wilcock and Mrs C. Woods.

Books consulted include:

Dunshaw, A Lancashire Background by T. W. Pateman (1948); *Blackburn As It Is* by P. A. Whittle; *Lays from Lancashire*, words by Nelson
Jackson with an introduction by the Rt Hon. Tom Shaw, PC, MP
(1930); *Life in a Cotton Town: Blackburn 1818–48* by Brian Lewis

(Carnegie Press, 1985); *Lancashire* by J. D. Marshall (City and County Histories, David & Charles, Newton Abbot, 1974); *Puppets through Lancashire* by Walter Wilkinson (1936); *Tacklers' Yarns* by Owd Shuttle (2nd edition, 20th thousand, *c.* 1923); *The Spinning Mule* (Bolton Metropolitan Borough Arts Department); *The Blackpool Story* by Brian Turner and Steve Palmer (1981); *Accrington: Chronology and Men of Mark* by R. S. Crossley (1924); *The Two-Up and Two-Downer* by Jim Partington (St Ann's Press, Park Road, Altrincham, 1972); *Automatic Weaving: the Northrop System* (Blackburn, 1940); *Children's Employment Commission Report, 1841,* John L. Kennedy on employment of children and young persons in print grounds and miscellaneous trades in Lancashire.

A personal note. It has taken a considerable time to compile this book and a number of people whose lives and thoughts are reflected here have died. They include Jack Thornley (*The monumental pudding*); Norman Bentley, journalist, a great story-teller and a splendid companion; and Bill Swift, a close friend (*Whatever happened to the stock pot?*). I hope that what I have written perpetuates their memories and reminds others of their great merits and enthusiasms.

GEOFFREY MATHER

Illustrations

The photographs of mill workers in this book are reproduced by courtesy of the Harris Museum and Art Gallery, Preston. The cartoons are by Ivan Frontani.

1

THE END OF AN EIRE

Probably, by the time the North of England is in industrial ruin, we shall be able to beat the world at table tennis.

J. B. Priestley

... a terrible heap of houses and buildings with blackened church spires standing here and there, and hundreds of high chimneys belching forth like fiery dragons, till the whole place looks like a city sunk in a sea of smoke. Amidst that sickening jerry-jumble of cheap bricks and cheaper British industry, over 100,000 men, women and children toil and exist, sweating in the vast hot, stuffy mills and sweltering forges ... growing up stunted, breeding thoughtlessly, dying prematurely, knowing not nor dreaming of aught better than this shrieking, steaming sphere of slime and sorrow.

Description of Bolton in the 1890s

LANCASHIRE IS TOO DIVERSE a county to be described easily, and Yorkshire even more so. Their rivalries are a myth, which cricket likes to perpetuate. Both have a gritty temperament. The monosyllabic gruntiness of the Yorkshire Dalesman (described by James Herriot) is how I remember my uncles in Lancashire. But Doncaster man is not Dales man. And Ribble man is not Manchester man. So we cannot be too sweeping in our assumptions. Humour is the thread that binds. It is self-deprecating. It dares to humiliate the teller, or the teller's friends. Such bravery is easily come by. By comparison, the South is secretive, and inhibited.

But if you expose Southerners to this humour, they fall for it; their inhibitions evaporate.

So there is hope for them, or us.

I am concerned here, principally, with Lancashire, although most of what is in this book reflects the whole of the North. The county, like a microcosm of Yorkshire, is all things: benign with moorland and mountain, rich soils and the rural webs of hamlets; and brooding as it bears evidence in land and water of industrial spoilage. At its worst, it is grey, forbidding, harsh to the eye and enervating of spirit; at its best, it is pristine and mellow, a benediction to the senses. It has always been so. The mythology of the South is that Lancashire is a monument to pollution. This myth was born because of the peculiarly depressing vistas from many tracks of British Rail: flat caps and satanic mills, derelict cars and purple weeds. A simplistic vision.

Many places in Lancashire exist as neighbours, but contradict each other violently: Blackpool, for instance, is garish, strident, bold, brash, a boozy old uncle of a place with the smell of vinegar about him, a cheerful brawler; whereas nearby Lytham St Annes is a maiden aunt, fussy about the habits of those around her, her nose in the air, her linen crisp. Comedian Les Dawson made his home there and said, not altogether seriously, 'Change does not come easily. I find that appealing. It is Waiting for Godot time. And Ansdell is so quiet it would send a glass eye to sleep. There was a bit of a traffic jam, only four cars, and this old colonel said, "It's getting more and more like Singapore".'

Bacup no more understands Barrow-in-Furness than it does Benares. Liverpool and Manchester go their separate ways, with different pursuits, cultures and accents, and long, long ago the writer, Haslam Mills, travelling between these two disparate places, noted 'the peculiar vacancy of view from the carriage window as the train travels across fields which seem to have no purpose except to hold the earth together and grow celery ... a frontier between two cities which are not, and never really have been, on speaking terms.'

Liverpool has a genius for words, which it chooses to misunder-stand. A leading solicitor there told me that police were 'the best detergent against crime'. A professional man said of a meal that it consisted of 'silver steak with all the tarnishings'. The same man, at a gathering where the chairman declared, 'That was mooted at the last meeting,' said, 'Oh yes, I remember that moot.' Someone he knew 'did not masturbate his food properly'. A deserted Adelphi Hotel was 'like a Muslim'. A man in court was 'found a pound'. Ford Consuls are Ford Consulars, and Anglias are Angulars. One supposes they represent the end of an Eire. Liverpool remains a standing monument to the tortured tonsil.

History marches grandly in such places as Lancaster and Clitheroe with their castles, and in Ribchester ('It costs 8*d.* to get a shilling out of Ribchester') with its broad river and echoes of Roman legions: the heavy imprint of the industrial revolution is elsewhere.

I am particularly familiar with Clitheroe, since I worked there as a young journalist and found it to be, as it remains, a place of brown boots, good tweed, and a suggestion of deep country class. Clitheroe's wine shops are a barometer of affluence. Some of its citizens proceeded on a daily basis, in my recollection, from a relaxed discussion of the weather, to morning coffee, to ram lambs and long tups, to shearlings (sheep), and thence to afternoon tea and, if the mood took them, a thoughtful contemplation of nature's changing face before supper and early bed. A senior journalist here prodded cows' udders at agricultural shows, a deeply meaningful act whose significance escaped me.

Lancashire, then, can present a pleasant face, and behind this benevolence are evidences of the grinding teeth, the cogs of industry, and these are in the East Lancashire heartlands where muck and mill and the pursuit of profit did their best and their worst to place and to people.

This book is a small pebble in the river of Lancashire life, designed to impede the current temporarily and in a modest way, so that something of the past – and in particular the humour of that past – is retained for those who find pleasure in recollection.

It began life as a selection of tacklers' tales, simple cotton-mill jokes which usually have evidence of truth, however unlikely the proposition. Then it spread, and took on age of its own.

Tacklers' tales were based on gormlessness, but they mutated in various ways. The humour was adapted for professional stage acts. In addition, as education improved, so did the deadpan humour. From being unintentional it became highly intentional and perceptive, but the basic form was retained. It is now sprinkled through half the conversations of the county as a matter of course. At its core is a sense of the ridiculous.

The kind of humour Lancashire generates grew from its social base: from the hardships and industry of the past. So history and industry are reflected in this book, too, though not in a comprehensive

way. Rather, I chose bits here and there, a pot pourri, in the belief
that an amalgamation of small dishes would provide, in the end, a
rounded meal: an essence, a whiff of what was and is.

Once, then, Lancashire had a cotton rather than a textiles industry
and tacklers were an essential part of it. Women operated the looms.
Men were called to repair mechanical defects. The men were overlookers, but were always known as tacklers (although at some late
stage, they acquired a fancier name which I, in common with most
other people, now thankfully forget), and tacklers were assumed, not
always correctly, to be undiscerning souls lacking rational perception.

The ground rules for delivering tacklers' humour were (and still
are) that sharpness of mind should, at all times, be concealed. There
should be no suggestion of cleverness. There should be an element

Tacklers and overlookers at a Lancashire mill.

of the ridiculous, but the joke should fall just short of being un-
believable. The words should be delivered seriously, unemotionally,
in the manner of a Les Dawson. The form of that humour was best
reflected in music halls when the manufacture of cotton was one of
the country's main industries. Tacklers might not be mentioned
specifically, but the jokes were interchangeable between them and
the comedians.

> So I came to Oldham, pouring rain, knocked on this door.
> Landlady said, 'Yes?'
> I said, 'Can I stay here for t'week?'
> 'Aye,' she says, 'you can, but you'll get dam'd wet.'

That joke was used by a comedian of, I would guess, the 'forties,
who read his prompts from the back of a six-foot plank of wood,
which he had with him on stage.

Gormlessness, or the assumption of it, has always been an art
form. It was the rich earth of many a remembered harvest of humour
and for Britain at large there were strong elements of it in Morecambe
and Wise. (Eric Morecambe, hearing the emergency siren of a
speeding vehicle: 'He'll never sell ice-cream driving at that speed.')

In Hollywood, Stan Laurel, originally Arthur Stanley Jefferson, a
Lancastrian from Ulverston, was, and remains, the world's greatest
exponent of the mayhem of innocence. Compare his face with that
of George Formby: were they not seeking a similar effect? The tackler
effect? If some lunar visitor were to arrive and come across a collection
of tacklers' tales, would he not match them with a picture of Stan
Laurel and say, 'That is the perfect tackler's face'? Lancashire would
recognise Laurel immediately as a man who, in other circumstances,
might well have been a mill overlooker, whereas Oliver Hardy, born
near Atlanta, Georgia, could only have reflected one's conception of
a mill manager or owner.

With all the laughter around, there is, yet, a tendency to think of
industrial Lancashire as a place of perpetual suffering. 'Even on a
sunny day, with blue skies,' said one distinguished expatriate, 'you
can look at them and know that, inside their souls, it is pouring
down.' I am uncomfortable with that assumption. The Lancastrian
face is frequently a curtain behind which there is a three-act comedy.
There are those who would give birth to a joke if the heavens were
roaring and the earth tumbling beneath their feet.

I was a child of the 'thirties, when suffering was supposedly endemic, yet my recollection is of other things. A child sees what is. He has nothing with which to compare that vision. Too young to have a past, and not old enough to put the present into perspective, he accepts the things around him as the only things there are. My parents, and other older people, no doubt suffered through fear, insecurity and, for all I know, lack of money, but they were my shield against such misfortunes. I was a child and, therefore, all was simple. I saw warmth, friendship, neighbourliness, and I heard laughter. There were many like me.

Suffering is no part of my memory. Memories are of hot potatoes straight from the oven, eaten in the street on Thursday mornings; the black-peas cart making its rounds by night; the intimacy of terraced houses; mill chimneys rearing and billowing their hot breaths at the sky (one could count more than forty from Church cricket field).

The first sight of Blackpool Tower after a long winter was a moment sublime in everyone's experience. There was nothing to equal it because it was the apex of all existence; or so we thought.

Out of living memory now are the industrial riots and the deaths, the deep pain of the past. Those who endured this torment are long gone. My generation can have little idea of how they felt. We live in better times and all is relative. People now are suffering if they do not have fitted carpets, their own spectacles (my father, and many like him, made do with those left behind by deceased relatives, an act of fiscal prudence rather than necessity), paid-for haircuts, a refrigerator (in the 'thirties, no house needed a refrigerator because every house already was one), a television set, a washing machine, a bath that does not have to hang outside on a nail, or an interior lavatory … If someone in the 'thirties had mentioned Andrex, people would have thought it was a Greek god. I recall a joke about a child taking toilet rolls back to a shop and asking for the money to be returned. 'Why, is there something wrong with 'em?' 'No, but my dad says our visitors are not coming now.'

Most people I know had none of these things, but they would not have regarded their absence as deprivation. They would have been affronted by any such suggestion. The old saying that what you never have you never miss is true enough. People were hard on themselves and took pride in their ability to face problems. Those who complained over-much were 'marred', softies lacking moral backbone.

To go to bed in winter was to experience the lifestyle of an Eskimo. Frost patterns of intricate shape decorated the interior of house windows. You helped these designs along by scraping at them with your fingernails. The beds were freezing apart from one tiny part covered by a hot water bottle. You curled up like a foetus and shook. If the discomfort of one position became too much to bear, you moved your feet to the foot of the bed inch by freezing inch. The more prudent among us kept our socks on, together with anyone else's if they were lying around. If we switched on the light, breath was clearly visible.

There were coal fires in old iron ranges, but they never, in my recollection, roared up the chimney like tigers, as I have seen miners' fires roar. They flickered like old aunts, in a delicate state of health, sickly from birth, and when they needed replenishing, the coals were applied one by one in tiny pieces. A brain surgeon would have recognised the delicacy of the operation: a piece here, a piece there.

In spite of the meagreness of the warmth, women's legs were invariably mottled by exposure to heat and their backs froze. The black
iron shone. When visitors arrived, they were invited to draw up a
chair to the fire, but there was precious little room there in a tight
semi-circle of family. A child had to fight for an inch of spare space.
Burning coal was a living picture of pattern and movement, endlessly
fascinating for those who wished to just sit and stare. You could see
faces dancing there in the flames, strange animals, whole moving
landscapes. If much of television had half coal's fascination it would
be better entertainment than it is.

Cold fingers ached like tooth cavities and the skin of hands cracked
(unless they happened to have the benefit of an old tobacco tin,
pierced by small holes and filled with smouldering cotton wool).
Everyone had chilblains. It might be more accurate to say that the
chilblains had people.

Even in the early 'sixties, Lord Birkett, the great Lancastrian judge
and advocate, read in bed to the accompaniment of 'one bar of an
electric fire and a thick sweater'. There were other suggestions for
reading in bed. The Times correspondence column listed some: 'A
woollen ski cap, a Shetland shawl, mittens secured at the wrists by
means of rubber bands ... Learn Braille and read under the bed
clothes ... A thick cardigan got into the wrong way round and pulled
well up under the chin.'

Summers were hotter than they now are, of course: they always
are in the memory. And the sun baked dog excrement white, so that
a child I knew confused it with discarded toffee. Just the once, that
is. We sat on the edge of pavements and pricked tar bubbles when
the weather was fine. There was usually water inside the bubbles.
When it rained, we raced matchsticks in the torrents. As a more
revealing alternative, we used to unravel old golf balls to find the sac
of something heavy and glutinous at the centre.

Great grey, human tides used to turn up for Lancashire League
cricket matches and people knocked on house doors asking for glasses
of water. Every ground had its wag, who yelled at the players, and
every wag had his followers.

People talked to each other endlessly; long evenings of talk. As a
child, it is what I remember – the droning of voices in my grandmother's home as a backdrop to my own gathering waves of tiredness.
Without an ounce of privilege to their names, the aunts and uncles

were, surprisingly, I feel, all Conservatives in that terraced house in Duke Street, Oswaldtwistle. Anyone not Conservative was assumed to want something for nothing, the ultimate sin. My grandmother owned her own home, which possibly accounts for the Conservatism, lived on a pension of ten shillings a week (50p), and counted her blessings one by one as the Sunday school tune taught her to do. We knew a lot about what Jesus could do for multitudes in the way of loaves and fishes, and grandmothers were expected to have a similar surprising facility. Jesus, we knew, was gentle, meek and mild, so He must have been more like us than He was a mill manager. If someone had written our Good Book, it would have said, 'In the beginning was the mill, and the mill was with God and the mill *was* God. Fifty-one weeks did they labour, creating sheet and shirt, and on the fifty-second, they rested.'

Everyone in town went on holiday in the same week of the year, leaving it to the occasional dog's bark and blowing papers. No-one went to Spain unless they were Spaniards or freedom fighters. In those days, no-one would have known in which direction that country lay. It is said of someone who set out from Blackburn to walk around the world, seen off by a large crowd, that he was not sure which direction to take at the start. Would it be through Bolton, or Preston? He settled for Accrington, and so far as I know got no further. Accrington was, presumably, the edge of his known world, an outer rim beyond which he would tumble into the void; unless, that is, the country was engaged in a major war, in which case the authorities kindly decided the route and provided, too frequently, only a one-way ticket.

Honeymooners called Blackpool 'the West Coast'. It looked better when so described in the local newspapers' wedding reports. You booked and paid for a room at a boarding house and crammed in as much of the family as you could. My paternal grandmother, a blunt woman of awesome energy, who would not tolerate a book in the house because she regarded reading matter as a form of mental pollution, took her large family to Blackpool and gathered up, in the process, a neighbour's child who happened to be playing in the street as the party was leaving.

'Are all these yours?' asked the disbelieving landlady. 'Aye,' said my grandmother, 'all mine apart from this – she's one I'm aunt to.'

Cotton became textiles. Tacklers became like eagles, Wales, whales and rain forests: they were in need of preservation from the encroaching new age. The clattering, dusty looms vanished, together with many mills. Mill owners with hard hats and turnip watches gave way to conglomerates, and instead of factory whistles, buttons were pressed in London to herald multi-shift working. My father said the world as we knew it ended when mills installed canteens and fitted carpets. He was right. People at the other side of the world took on the burden of the flying thread and now consider the terrible price of progress. Terraced streets filled with cars of dubious vintage which, initially, were like churchgoers: they only 'went' on Sundays. Outside lavatories, with their squares of torn newspaper impaled on rusty nails, were dismantled and there was no longer any confusion about whether 'the long drop' referred to the inner workings of the privy or the gallows. Chilblains retreated as background heating advanced. Radiators sprouted to leak on patterned carpets. Rickets, product of inadequate diet, vanished and people no longer had legs like goalposts. The consumption was no longer a disease but a measure of things consumed. Debt, once secret and dreaded, a thing of deep shame, was encouraged by financial institutions as an expression of virtue to be advertised in newspapers. People whose banks had been tea caddies acquired accounts at those high-street premises where they take your money without fuss, but check very carefully before giving it back, the assumption being that their honesty is without question whereas yours is open to doubt.

The street-corner clogger vanished, his mouth full of tacks, and children were deprived of an absorbing pastime: that of skidding their clog irons along paving stones to make sparks. When people were dying they did not assume, as my dying maternal grandmother did, that a glass of stout given iron by the insertion of a red-hot poker would reverse the process of dissolution. Doctors and preachers, long revered for their learning and ability to save you first in this life, then in the next, lost status as education improved. Dentists began to assume that if you required an extraction, anaesthetic was not an option but a necessity. If I had a tooth extracted, my father used to say, 'Tell him not to put stuff on.' Stuff killed pain, but he reckoned that as anaesthetic wore off you got pain anyway, so why pay the extra?

I do not miss what people call the poverty, although I would have described it as a severe lack of money. I am delighted that 'ordinary'

Northerners are to be found holidaying all over the world. I regret that communities are not so close and mutually dependent as they were. I applaud the greater affluence, though I am not sure that it has produced a greater virtue. On the contrary, I would imagine that in some ways, affluence is capable of both expanding and diminishing people. Those with more to spend are, not infrequently, people with less to give.

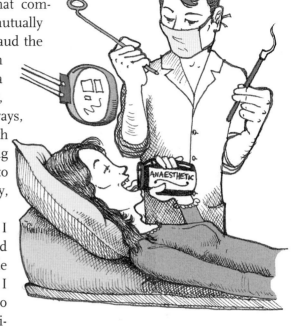

I miss the old music halls. I miss the smell of oranges and attendants with stockings made from holes loosely intertwined. I miss the orchestra leader who occasionally turned to the audience during what he considered the good bits to nod his head and smile approvingly. The shine of his black suit matched that of his black hair, and when he went home on the last tram, he sat on top, at the front, belching occasionally, and apologising each time to the entire cargo of ale-carrying humanity. What his stomach lacked in gastric order was balanced by his unfailing courtesy. To underline his regrets, he would take out his fiddle and play a lively tune.

This, then, was the era of the tackler and of the tacklers' tales. This was the era of character and characters both on and off stage. I would like to introduce both.

2

A VISION OF TIMES PAST

THE OVERLOOKER, or tackler, should be a trained mechanic rather than one who works by rule of thumb. He must 'tune' looms rather than 'tackle' them. That is to say, he must work to definite measurements rather than rough and ready ideas, to a sixteenth of an inch rather than the thickness of a penny. This applies more, of course, to the settings of the automatic motions than the running of the loom. But the ordinary loom tackler has developed his skill on individual lines rather than mechanical. Every loom in his set is different and has to be treated differently as a result. He has to 'humour' each one of his looms as he gets to know it, and his knowledge is largely instinctive as a result. He will listen to, and feel, a loom when 'tackling' it, and very often is unable to say what it is necessary to do to it; and yet he will go and do it and then not be sure exactly what effect it has had.

Such a method is useless with automatic machinery; and the automatic loom tuner must study the mechanism of one loom, master its motions and their settings, and then apply this knowledge to all the looms in his section alike.

Automatic Weaving: The Northrop System, Blackburn, 1940

In the olden days, the only requirement of a tackler was a big shoulder to carry warps and a big hammer to do the fitting jobs.

C. B. Fawcett of Nelson, a tackler for thirty-six years

Once, men, women and children hurried to their work on a winter's morning at 6 a.m. and the sight of the mill tacklers, lined up in the entrance lobby, waiting to pounce on late comers, led to a good deal of bitterness in the sheds, especially among women operatives. It was the poor weaver who suffered most fear, for the good four-loom worker cared for no tackler living, and could always be trusted to fling back as good as she received.

Tacklers' Yarns, collected and edited by 'Owd Shuttle', c. 1924

Tackler to weavers at a Preston mill between the wars: 'If that door could weave, it would mean as much to me as any of you.'

Recalled by Mrs C. Woods, Penwortham, Preston

The reading of [tacklers'] jokes brought to me a kind of homesickness. I could hear the sudden roar of the machinery as the weaving shed door opened, and feel the blast of warm air and the peculiar weaving-shed smell, quite different from any other smell on earth. I could see the men and women at the looms, the most skilful and independent of their class in the world. I remembered the hundreds of good stories I have heard in the shed, for every day brings a new one in all the thousands of weaving sheds in Lancashire.

Tom Shaw, MP, in a foreword to Laws from Lancashire
by Nelson Jackson, c. 1930

3

AN ENIGMA ON ICE

*H*UMOUR at the amateur level is best identified for me in the person of a stout little pudding of a man with a nasal drip of the kind provided by winter, not hospitals. Joe Tomlinson was his name. Although there were, perhaps, others no less perceptive, or capricious, he was distinguished in his anonymity to the point where many considered him unique. He was neither affluent nor prominent in the public affairs of Darwen, but he was the kind of man who remained on the palate, like a good wine, or (occasionally) like an irritant pip when the grape has gone: a generic type of Lancastrian, predictable in movement, but never in thought.

I met him in a pub and he looked like a hundredweight of small coal in black coat and bowler, the drip in a permanent state of indecision on the end of his questing nose.

'Aye,' he was saying to a couple of lorry drivers from Liverpool, 'I saw this lass in Woolworth's. Lovely lass. I followed her across t'circus [the town centre] and up t'long lane, o'er t'bridge, and then I ketched her. Aye, I ketched her behind t'hen cabins.'

The lorry drivers conjured up this steamy scene, then one said, 'How long ago was that?'

I thought he said it patronisingly. He was innocent of all knowledge of having been led into a trap. Joe looked to be a hundred years old at the time and was ripe as mature Stilton.

'Oh,' said Joe screwing up his eyes, pummelling his mind, sorting through the cobwebs of its innermost recesses, and finally retrieving the information he required – 'must have been a fortnit since.'

A BBC man once went in search of him. 'He will be in the pub,' said a friend. 'What,' said the BBC man, a prude one imagines, 'at half-past three?' This was the days of three o'clock closing, but Joe was not inhibited by time if he could find a friendly landlord. He had found one that day and was drinking rum and hot water, on his own. The BBC man began to dredge for anecdotes.

'I used to make rope,' said Joe. 'There was a fellow asked me to make a noose. I told him it would be 1s. 3d. and he paid me in mouldy pennies. Well, I worried about him a bit. He could have been hanging himself. So I tracked him down to a tent. I had to pay 2d. to go in. He had this rope on show and said it was the rope that hanged Charlie Peace. Aye, he did.'

The BBC man listened a bit more then left, saying he could not have Joe on his show because he was unpredictable. So he was. Joe saw a laundromat for the first time, watched the clothes turning around behind the circular windows and grumbled, 'If that's television, I reckon nowt of it.'

When a constable said he was booking Joe for having a chimney on fire, Joe said, 'It's nowt to what it was when t'inspector was here.' The constable put his book away. There had been no inspector.

Joe joined the Special Constabulary during the last war and the police force was never the same again. 'Where have you been?' said the desk man when Joe arrived back late one night from patrol.

'Park,' said Joe, 'like you told me.'

'Never,' said the desk man. 'The inspector's been looking for you for hours and he couldn't find you.'

'That's funny,' said Joe. 'I've been in t'park all night.'

'Which park?'

'Park Hotel,' said Joe, straight-faced. 'Isn't that what you meant?'

He boarded a late-night tram in uniform and the conductor said, 'I'm glad you're here. Fellow upstairs won't pay his fare.'

'Leave him to me,' said Joe.

'Now,' he said to a labourer who had fire in his eyes, strong drink on his breath, and an open shirt revealing a torso normally seen only on a Sumo wrestler, 'what's all this about you not payin' your fare?'

The labourer eyed Joe with scant interest. 'I'm just not,' he said.

'No,' said Joe, 'and I don't blame you.'

He fished in his pocket for 3*d*., went downstairs, handed the money to the conductor, and said, 'Theer, you don't know how to treat 'em.'

He never seemed to have moved from the pub corner when I met him, black suit to green plush, and it was in that same position that a friend found him.

'It's not Joe Tomlinson?'

'It is.'

'You remember me, Joe. It must be twenty-five years since I saw you.'

'Aye,' said Joe. 'What are you havin', then?'

'I'll have a large scotch with you, Joe.'

Joe pondered this request, then said, 'Well, I hope it's another twenty-five years ...'

Darwen slopes are built more for goats than people, and in winter one can observe its inhabitants sliding about all over the place, out of control until the onset of Spring. Joe and a mutual friend named Norman Bentley drank in a place high above the town and later, since Joe was incapable of walking the treacherous surfaces, Norman offered to drag him by the heels. Joe agreed, since it was the closest he would get to a taxi. Norman removed his own shoes so as to get a better grip on the ice (he called it 'purchase', not 'grip') and was depressed to hear them sliding away in the dark towards the town centre. He had been dragging Joe for a while when, from the direction of the ground, came Joe's disembodied voice.

'Hey,' he said, 'I'll tell thee what, Norman.'

'What?'

'Whatever tha does, don't set off at t'run.'

Darwen was and, I hope, is (though I ceased to know it) a town of characters, a main-road sausage through a sandwich of hills where, for much of the year, the clouds weep. There was a dentist who cut off people's ties when he had a drink or two; a managing director who pulled out a wad of pound notes as thick as a navvy's wrist and said, 'I suppose I'm carrying more money than anyone else here?' only to beaten in fivers by a scrap metal dealer. There was an Irish doctor, Dennis, who could look you straight in the eye, as he did me, and say, 'A fellow like you could go' – here, a click of the fingers – 'just like that.' He went just like that himself, as it happens.

Joe was the catalyst, the permanence, the elusively unpredictable in a bunch of like and lively minds. He died and left behind the vibrant essence of himself in the memories of others.

So much for the astute amateur affecting gormlessness for the amusement of family and friends. There also had to be the professionals who excelled in this great well of humour.

4

THE NIGHT THE QUEEN
SAID 'SHUT UP!'

THE NORTH, and Liverpool in particular, have probably produced more comedians than any other part of the land. Some transplant and thrive: Formby, Askey, Tarbuck, Dawson, Morecambe *et al*. Others have been too long in the soils of their birth to survive the upheaval. The two comedians who most deeply represented their roots and their class were Albert Modley and Frank Randle, both brash, both loved, both more at home on stage than anywhere else, although Randle also made films which appeared to have come fresh out of someone's back yard, having displaced the brush and shovel in the process.

Albert, in truth, was a Yorkshireman, but he chose to live in Morecambe and his humour was as close to Burnley's as it was to Batley's.

Frank Randle, was from Standish, Wigan area, and once, in his youth, sold 't'finest oranges in Wiggin at t'middle of Chorley market site proper next to t'pump.' He always appeared on stage without teeth. He would stagger on carrying the sort of red lamp found near street excavations.

'Look what some dam'd fool left in t'road,' he would say, and the theatre would erupt with joy at the sight of him, not so much because it was funny – which it was – but because any tackler in the audience might have said the same thing in identical circumstances.

Randle had a sketch in which he played a character celebrating his hundredth birthday. He would sit there, surrounded by relatives, being fawned upon, and his mind would appear to wander, vague and without reason, until in some flash of reality he would leap onto a table, grab his old army cutlass, and cry: 'Come among me – I've had eight on t'end of this at once.'

When an old girl friend, long past her prime, arrived on stage he chased her off and reappeared grasping her undergarments. His stage wife glared accusingly. He was all innocence. 'They just came off in my hand, love.'

When, at the end, he and his partner lit the candles to go upstairs to bed, tears rolled in the audience, for Randle's was comedy and drama at the same time, and here was the man's greatness. He was as much actor as comedian, strong and inimitable in his own right. When a theatre annoyed him, he went up in an aircraft and bombed it with toilet rolls. He was invariably vulgar. He would appear on stage carrying a beer bottle, take a swig, then belch loudly. 'Aye,' he would say, 'there's eight of them in every bottle.'

He would appear in bathing costume. 'By God, that watter was cold. When I came out I didn't know whether my name was Angus or Agnes.' Brash and vulgar, then, and noble, too; daring for his time, but sensitive, a regional comedian of the type that declined as theatres faded and television grew in strength.

And so to Modley.

Albert was fifty-six when I met him, full of wheezy laughs and living by Morecambe promenade. He was funny without trying to be so on occasions. He said things like, 'He was unmatured for t'job' (referring to one of a new breed of comedian), or, 'That's the most miserablest time I ever had.'

Predictably, perhaps, he referred to radio as wireless, and to some, even at that time, he was an anachronism. He was much more gentle than Randle. We sat in his front room sharing a common joy at past times and good stories and at intervals a woman he failed to introduce would poke her head around the door and say, sharply, 'Why are you telling him all that? Why don't you talk about now? Why is it always the past?' And I smiled, but I was thinking, 'Why don't you push off, and why don't you realise that this man is unique and great and warm and memorable and precious, so that he can say what he likes?'

See him set there, all square and capped, on stage and you were able to observe every echo of humour that ever came out of the vast caverns of the Northern region. You could peel him like an onion, each layer rich and revealing and satisfying because he represented several generations of thought and each one was, and is, being lost in the new ethic of international sameness.

Lacking the music hall and that remarkably English idiosyncrasy known as the fol de rols, the new comics began to look alike, dress alike, and tell the same jokes. Nothing funny ever happened to them on the way to the theatre because they had never performed in one. There is not a comic in the land who could have described, in all seriousness, a Royal Command Performance like this:

> So the Queen and Duke of Edinburgh were in this box and there's another box at the other side of the theatre, built to balance things, and make it look nice, and everyone comes on and bows to Her Majesty, but I don't. I bows to the wrong box, and then I look up and say, 'Have they gone?'
>
> Well, then I turn round and say, 'Ah, there they are. How are you?' as if I'd known them all my life. I forget to bow, but lovely. I don't overdo it. I crack a gag about our mayor not wearing a chain – we let him run loose. Well it got a heck of a laugh, so when we were lined up afterwards to meet the Queen and Duke, I went first.
>
> Anyway, it's a bit nervy-wracky, but they're so good to talk to. She says, 'I've thoroughly enjoyed your performance' (she'll say that to all of 'em) but anyhow she says, 'I've had a good laugh,' and the Duke says, 'Yes, jolly good.' She says, 'But I didn't understand why you say the mayor doesn't wear a chain because he does.' She says, 'I distinctly saw it and it had a ship on with a crest and a thing like a net, what they call' – oh, what did she say? – 'something they go shrimping with.' And the Duke says, 'I always thought they went with a net,' so she says, 'Shut up.'
>
> Well, I'm stood there, so I say, 'That were just a bit of fun,' and she says, 'Oh,' she says, 'well, I thoroughly enjoyed it,' and he says, 'Very good,' and there's the band leader, Jack Hylton, going like this [here, an urgent movement of hands], like, go on, go on, and don't be all night. And I had no lead to tell me I'd finished so we went on talking. Course, when I go away everybody's breaking their necks – like, what did she say? I tried to tell them the best way I could and cameras were going and they said, 'We don't know whether you'll see this reported tomorrow because there's this national newspaper strike.' And we never did.

Albert's phraseology was always delicately tinged by beauty. Describing a fellow comic, slightly blue: 'He is a bit, but not too.' He always laughed a lot off stage and on. The laughs, born somewhere around the fourth rib down, bounced around quite a bit before emerging, all throaty, as if a lozenge would not do any harm. He became one of the few men around who could laugh like that and make it an affirmative at the same time:

'Oh-ah-ah-ah-ha-ha-aaaye-oh-aye.'

I asked him which kind of humour he preferred.

'Daft things about silly pals I have. *So he knocks on this door and the fellow shouts, "I'm out," but he knew he wasn't.* Or, *He stood in front of this mirror with his eyes shut and a friend said, "What's up wi' you?" and he said, "I'm seeing what I look like when I'm asleep."* '

I found it impossible to watch Albert on stage and not feel an initial anticipation, a sense of history, a hint of nostalgia, because he became the last of a great and traditional line. He would stand, squat and jowly, pretending to be a tram driver, using drum cymbals to imitate the controls, juddering his body and calling to someone imaginary on the line ahead:

'What do you mean, where am I going? I'm going' – here the head craning outwards and upwards to glimpse a non-existent destination board on the exterior of the tram – 'I'm going to DU-PLI-CATE.'

Albert was around show business so long that he came in for the second house: the great club boom. He started in clubs during the 1926 strike, progressed to theatres and panto (thirteen pantos with Francis Laidler) and films (*Up for t'Cup, Take Me to Paris, Bob's Your Uncle, Bob's Shop*), and so back to clubs.

'There's only one way to start in this theatre business,' he said, 'and that's in concert party. That breaks 'em in. I had eight or nine years of it, every summer. They were all funny sketches, comics quick on and off, and you didn't bother about scenery, lighting, you know? We just used to dress up. A right schooling is that.'

One of Modley's first engagements after leaving the railway, where he was a porter 'promoted from Otley to Bradford', was in Limerick. He was in a double act, The Two Eddies.

Limerick, oh Gawd, it was murder for me because they didn't know what I was talking about. As far as Ireland goes, I wouldn't mind a holiday, but I wouldn't go to work there again. Not Limerick. They threw everything. We used to get so that we daren't go on. Terrible, two of us trembling in the wings. We were supposed to do about eight minutes and we were doing three. The boss would say, 'You haven't been on, have you?' and we'd say, 'We have – we've had enough.'

'Look out,' we'd say – halfpennies, pennies, owt would come. We thought, Roll on Saturday! and the digs – cor, oh boy; hardly any lights, tumbling up steps into a cold bedroom. I'll tell you when it was – Limerick races. Never forget it as long as I live. Everything closed that day. 'You'll have a real time there,' everybody was telling us. It was the most miserablest time we ever had because we had nowt much, we couldn't afford to go to t'races, and we couldn't bet because we didn't know anybody, and they wouldn't speak to us much because as soon as you opened your mouth – English, ugh! And the pubs, clubs, every one closed. Couldn't get a drink of anything. By God, aye.

Limerick was not without its troubles for the show's organiser.

> He was giving record players away in talent contests. Well, anyway, he was supposed to be. But the Customs had not let them through, and he only had one. Anyway, a kid won it and he had to take it back off the child for the second house and that's where the bother started.
>
> Half the kids were waiting at the stage door. The organiser told the kid back-stage, 'Customs are not letting any record players through, love,' but the kid didn't know what he was saying.
>
> Second house, same again. By Tuesday or Wednesday we had to have the police there to help us, to see us home. Thursday, the gramophones came through. He billed it best way he could – 'All gramophones will be given away Thursday.' Friday, he was giving two away at once to show 'em how good he was, but it was too late then. Oh, Gawd, it was murder.

A little cult grew around Albert long after his peak. People phoned each other to say, 'He's on, Saturday night,' and radios untouched in years would burst into life at the throaty sound. When he appeared, thereafter, at one of the many Yorkshire clubs, they said, with warmth, 'If you live to be two hundred, you can come back here every year' – the ultimate accolade because that particular club was not given to fine words or behaviour. When a leading pop singer, a girl of some national reputation, appeared there, an official pounded the top of his table with a pint glass during her act and shouted, 'Best of order, please, ladies and gentlemen. Give the little cow a chance.'

'These younger comics,' said Albert, 'they think because they go into a club that they have to be filthy. But they haven't. The rougher the place, the more they hate filth. It's the lah-di-dah places where they love it. In London, they'll eat it. Surprising who went into working clubs eventually – oh, the lot. Frankie Howerd. People like that. Now from Howerd it isn't too bad and he doesn't do much of it, and you've known him so long, but if a young one went on and did it you'd think: Oh, geddoff. I do. I think: Go and have a bit of education. They're pros before they are pros, some of 'em. Now I don't crack blue gags. Not one. All simple. And they come quick. Like the old girl says, "My husband's very good, very kind to me. He holds the door open while I bring in the coal." Well, they make you laugh. You're forced to laugh because they come that quick.

'Frank Randle was another, but some thought him dirty. He was on his own was Frank, and he was clean to what they are now. He started about the same time as me with a trampoline act. By jove, he was strong. He only had to shake your hand and mean it and you realised how strong he was. Pity about Frank dying. He was good natured, but he drank quite a bit. When his wife was touring with him, he was all right.'

I can confirm the drinking. I once went home with Randle for a late-night chat after an hour or two in Blackpool Aero Club. He asked the barman to fill a light ale bottle with whisky. He re-capped the bottle and later drank from it by his own fireside while his wife, no doubt admiring the innocence of what appeared to be a habit, looked on.

I would like to have covered Randle and Modley in vinegar and pickled them as an example to the world. They established the simplest and most direct creed of them all: a pure and earthy creed. Albert summed it up. 'Hey,' he said, 'I'll tell you what, I do love a good laugh.'

There's a lot of back-chat at rehearsals. One comedian said that if an atom bomb dropped in Morecambe it would do £15-worth of damage.
John Hamp, Granada producer, talking of his show The Comedians

Worst experience I ever had. I turned up one night, half-past seven, at a club, puts me bag in the dressing room, goes to the bar, has a drink, and the trio come in and we all introduce ourselves. Bought them a drink; they bought me a drink. Then, about ten o'clock, they'd all finished their supper and they goes up and plays dance music. Then the organiser started having, like, raffles in a drum. I thought: It's getting a bit late here, half-past ten, so I said to the fellow, 'What time will I be on?' He said I'd better see such-a-body. So I gets on the phone to the agent, Bert, and I said, 'Bert, it's eleven o'clock and I haven't been on yet,' and he said, 'You're not on till tomorrow night.'

Mickey Finn, Liverpool comedian

I didn't really decide I was a comedian. I used to entertain lads in the army – songs at the piano and all this business, the odd gag, and I came out of the army and got a job selling Hoovers. I did part-time bits and it developed from there. I went to Hull to do a week's variety, about £14 for the week, bloody hard graft. On Thursday night, they were virtually throwing everything at me. I could not face them on the Friday, so I had a drink and when the curtain rose I started doing the dead-pan act, cheesed off with life generally, and to my bewilderment, there was a faint titter that grew to a crescendo.

Les Dawson

Clubs are great for keeping your feet on the floor. I worked with The Drifters when they first came here. A guy on stage said, 'Right, ladies and gentlemen – top of the bill here. They're not my cup of tea. In fact, the committee has gone over my head. The Drifters!' I nearly died.

Dudley Doolittle (real name Steve Pickering, from Rochdale),
comedian

5

STRAIGHT AS A PRINCIPLE

*T*HE INNER SPIRIT of the region, for me, resided in a grandmother who never sat any way but bolt upright, straight as a
principle. She is black in memory – black cotton stockings, black
cotton skirts – and she kept behind her brass-knobbed bed a painting
of some great-uncle who lost his eye at Waterloo. He was painted in
profile, his good eye to the fore.

She spread butter thinly, rather like a precision engineer with a
micrometer, made a penny last, maintained a clean tongue and a
clean table, wore a pinafore which she called a brat, had numerous
children whose names she never got right first time, and observed
at least twenty commandments, all good although only ten belonged
to God. I expect she assumed that when Moses originally carried
them down from the mountain he, being a man, became careless
and dropped one or two so that it was up to a woman to make up
the discrepancy.

I do not suppose that she was in any way different from thousands
of other Northerners caught in the warp and weft of a precarious
existence. Like them, she laughed a lot, and there was a particular
time, at Christmas, when the laughter became a danger to those
around her. She would thump the old board table with her fist at
the conclusion of some anecdote and all the plates would dance a
merry jig. It was disconcerting for the younger family members
present to see their turkey slices leaping up and down before their
eyes as if resurrection day had arrived and hallelujahs were called
for.

After such meals, she got out an old cylinder gramophone, with a
large horn to amplify its sound, and played such tunes as 'Silver
threads among the gold'. The slate-grey days of my early life. And
yet, through all the laughter, this Lancashire I knew was stark in
home and habit.

I came across a book on the history of the textiles industry, huge in fact, and it reminded me of my ancestry and touched the nerve ends of recollection:

> The masters would recommend that all their workpeople wash themselves every morning, but they shall wash themselves at least twice a week – Monday morning and Thursday morning – and any found not washed will be fined 3d. for each offence.

Here, another instruction to folk at the mill:

> All persons in our employ shall serve four weeks' notice before leaving their employ; but the proprietors shall, and will, turn any person off without notice being given.

There were, of course, good employers as well as bad, but even kindness had its abrasive qualities. I do not remember past employers in any detail apart from one, who used to give his servant half an apple for lunch, although my grandmother – a Howard who married a Morshead, he being an incomer from Cornwall, where they had a tin depression – would have remembered them well enough. She died in her eighties, the last loaf risen, the last prayer said, more than fifty years ago and rests for ever more in Great Harwood cemetery. Only now comes the realisation that I never knew her for what she really was.

And this is the way of things: first, the incomprehension of the very young; then their scepticism of older values, followed by rebellion, followed, in turn, by the dawn of understanding; and finally, everything full circle, the point at which they begin to comprehend their own parents at the precise time that their own children no longer comprehend them: the great wheel of inner conflict endlessly in motion down the centuries.

My grandmother would know hardship whereas I would see it only as excitement. There was the great strike when police horses around the mill pushed back crowds, and workers who were idle spat at those who were not idle. To me, a good time, because it represented a change of routine; to her, a graveyard of foundering hopes.

Dark mornings which were really late nights, and in them the scrape of clog on pavement, people working for shillings ... On Sundays, they went to church and said, straight-faced, 'The Lord is my Shepherd. I shall not want.' And this is the drama and contradiction of it, though there was little drama at the time. It was a fact,

a circumstance, and life was not without blessings. Health was regarded as the greatest, and there were times when there was not a
lot of that about.

There was nothing beyond those grey streets but Blackpool or
Morecambe, the further limits of life on earth. Nettle beer in Hey-
sham. Thursday a good day, baking day, when the big brown mixing
bowl perched before the fire. Rocking chairs, rag carpets, solid sideboards, kitchen with ceiling clothes racks, back yards, open doors,
neighbours, lorries with solid tyres ...

My grandmother was, then, of cotton and her children were of
cotton. Boys to the pit, girls to the mill. There was little else. She
referred to Disarella, meaning Disraeli, whom she had observed speaking on Accrington market place. She approved of him. I discovered
this affinity after I had written a piece in which I said that she found
him a disappointing fellow. Memory had played tricks and I was duly
put down by older relatives with better recollection. It was not her
opinion of Disraeli that I had, as a child, considered important. The
important thing was that, to me, he was history, deep and way back
beyond human recall and yet here was this old and ramrod woman
speaking of him casually as a contemporary.

In her children's time men in bowler hats ate black puddings from
street stalls. Their families lined up like marble statues to have their
likeness taken for posterity by cameras which betrayed the slightest
movements. Not a smile anywhere. To smile during a picture was
an insult to the art. Nowadays, everyone has to smile. Smiling is
obligatory. At what mysterious point in time did everything change?
Males in those days all seemed to look like Lord Kitchener: moustaches
taut, eyes stern. Kitchener's finger pointed accusingly at the nation
from posters. 'Your country needs you.' Who among them would be
disinclined to die on the Somme? A grim business.

When the Salvation Army first walked through Rishton, a place
which always looked uncertain about whether it wished to remain
where it was, the leader wore a top hat and the people kicked it all
around the village because it was judged to be a princely thing not
of this world.

Description of a weaving shed, 1873:

The overlooker is stimulating and driving the weavers all day long and
on making-up day, he goes round to each weaver with a slate and asks

the amount of the week's earnings. But before going round, he will generally ascertain, either from the books, or some other source, the highest earnings of any weaver in the shop and everyone who is not up to this mark will receive a severe chastisement at his hands.

Ah, the long history of the tackler! Mill rules, Haslingden, 1851:

Any person coming too late shall be fined as follows – for five minutes, 2d., ten minutes, 4d., 15 minutes, 6d. For any bobbins on the floor, 1d. for each bobbin. For waste on the floor, 2d. For any oil wasted or spilled on the floor, 2d., each offence, besides paying for the value of the oil.

Harshness at the mill, goodness in the streets. There was always a woman there to ease your birth and another to lay you out in death.

In between, the family, invariably large, so that the long board table creaked with Christmas and grandmother presided, a woman so awesome that her children, middle-aged themselves, called her 'Mama' to the end.

She recognised no sex distinction. When she took her youngest daughter and husband to live with her, she shouted regularly to them, 'Nine o'clock, lasses, and time for bed.' The world, in her opinion, was up to no good if it squandered good sleep for there was another early day ahead. How she knew what time it was is still a mystery to me. The sequence seemed to be that when the clock struck seven and the fingers stood at 9.25 it was, without doubt, nine o'clock. Or maybe eight. I am as confused now as I then was. Nowadays, everyone knows the time because they have radio and TV. In those days, people did not merely look at watches. They consulted them. Watches were profound instruments to be hauled slowly from waistcoat pockets by chain. A button had to be pressed to release a silver cover. Only then was The Face revealed. Only then could the delicate fingers be observed as cog and spring in delicate juxtaposition impelled their progress. The slow and sonorous tick and tock are fast vanishing from our world as quartz marches silently on. A house silent but for the heavy feet of a clock marching into infinity is a sure reminder of judgment to come. Preacher and clock-maker, I suspect, were in collusion.

We stoned Stanhillers (nearby villagers) across the delph and all the world was centred on this one place, Oswaldtwistle; all life there, with London a million miles away. It seemed good then. Few left it. The first to go abroad in any number died there. They were always fighting for freedom, of course. That is always a good thing to fight for, although I do not, to this day, know who defines what freedom is. I suspect it is just a word, like any other, but it has the merit of being emotive. I do not suppose those soldiers of freedom knew precisely where they were when the end came.

The teeth were indifferent, but the hearts were sound. The food was eyed with dedication and respect, not slung about, or left to birds. The starch was stiff and Sunday was the day when Mr Punker or Mr Cameron, preachers both at the Free Church of England, were the direct intermediaries between man and the Almighty, with not another soul between. A church worthy delivered Sunday school homilies on loaves and fishes and spat through his teeth, so that you were showered and instructed at one and the same time. Corn-coloured summers, wrestling in fields, 'puncing' matches where you held your opponent round the neck and kicked his shins with clogs until one or the other shouted, 'Enough!' And success if you could find it. Success being a sea you did not paddle in but sailed upon. Or butter spread thickly, as if there were plenty more where it came from.

> Should any tackler speak to a weaver about his earnings at any time or place, or speak unjustly when fetched to tackle the loom, we request such weaver at once to report ...

It all changed, of course. Unions gaining strength to the point (in industry in general) of becoming despotic in their turn. Few wear clogs now, but a little of the parsimony, a little of the respect for authority – these evidences remain to underscore the memories. Some Northerners still apologise when someone stands on their feet and they step beyond their county boundaries with apprehension. All is success now, or at least, relative success: weavers knowing St Tropez and Tuscany and the Algarve and the Costas. They drink wine now, and pubs make sure they get the worst of it at a price which makes them imagine they are getting the best of it.

Once, the likes of them grew cold before the hearth, gas lamps flickered on cobbles, and old drinking men in faded caps were ill against ginnel walls.

The affluence, such as it is, came too late for my grandmother, dead with her black stockings and her principles. When she was ill in her brass-knobbed bed, long before her terminal affliction, my father, who knew nothing of her ailments but only of her predicament, suggested champagne and chicken. It was a gesture as grand for its time as suggesting a specialist from China. She settled for stout, which was pragmatic, though drink was something of which she did not normally approve.

The house, her house, still stands, No. 8, in a row of such houses, seen by me at increasingly long intervals, and there are cars all over the place. Imagine that! Cars in the street! Nothing of her remains except her portrait.

My father, in turn, grew old, and at seventy-four went into hospital for observation. He, too, had his principles: stand on your own feet; don't ask for favours; work is good and idleness is unforgivable;

endure pain without complaint; be inferior to no man and look the lot in the eye. He had a sharp humour until his fifties, when it deserted him. His own father always liked to see the rest of the family off to bed and then sit quietly on his own, smoking a last pipe. The sons would suspend from their bedroom window a washer on a piece of string and swing it so that it tapped his downstairs window. Nothing was ever said, but the old man always retired to bed quickly when he heard the tapping.

I had agreed to be at my father's home by 9.30 a.m. to get him to hospital by 10 a.m. and I found him standing in front of the fire ready to deliver some heavy information. 'Now,' he said, 'this does not bother me at all. Going into hospital is nothing to me. There's no need to worry.' It occurred to me then, as it had occurred before, that there had never, at any time, been a great deal of communication between us. More a tacit understanding. Lancashire families were like that. He was a man of great emotion who was determined, at all times, never to show it. The depression years had scarred him. He occasionally recalled an old pit boss who never employed single men if he could help it, because he was more easily able to bully the married man and bend him to his will. My father had been a miner, a lorry driver and a newsagent: the latter was his great break for freedom, his chance to control his own future; but he never defeated the fear at the back of his mind that disaster was his near companion. I suspect that I inherited some of that fear.

He met life head on, charging at misfortune like a bull. I said, 'Why don't you bend? Flowers bend. Wheat bends. Otherwise, they would not survive.' He saw that as a great truth, and for once, was grateful for the advice. It was the only advice he ever took from me, and I do not recollect taking any from him.

By his own effort he had made himself financially independent of the threatening world and every penny of it came out of sweat. He felt joy in sweat. He lived his clichés. A fair day's work for a fair day's pay. Neither a borrower nor a lender be. Early to bed and early to rise (sometimes he opened his shop at 4.30 a.m. and closed it at 10 p. m.). He had enormous strengths but now, by his own standards, he was frail. The thing that brought brightness to his life was the thought that he could still hump more heavy boxes than a young man. His stories of great humpings tended to be repetitious and tedious.

'A load came in at nine o'clock,' he would say, referring to his part-time work after retirement, 'and I had it shifted by ten. They don't know how to work these days. Vincent [his boss] said to me, "Jim, you shouldn't do it. Let somebody help," and I said to Vincent, "I can't alter what's in my nature." '

My mother was frugal herself, investing her shillings. She would have liked a holiday, she said, but they had got out of the habit. They had not had a holiday in my recollection, although there was proof of holidays past in the old tin with its family pictures. These holidays were taken at seaside boarding houses, usually in Morecambe, where there was boxing, a sport my father liked. Groups of people were on the pictures, looking as if they had been laced up rigidly at birth from head to foot, remaining in that restricted state until they passed on, or over.

She had gone deaf and frail thinking about holidays she never had, and my father had said that when they retired they would sail round the world. But when the time came, they had lost the will, and it was never mentioned.

He had never, in his own words, 'ailed much'. Which is why this confrontation, this apparently simple scene – him in his cap standing by the fire in his terraced Oswaldtwistle home – was so charged with drama.

'Well then,' he said briskly. 'We'll get off to that hospital. Your mother's not coming. I've put my pyjamas on under this suit. Now when we get there, they might slip a bit and show below my pants. If they do, walk away and pretend you don't know me. I'll be all right. You can pick me up later.'

I nodded. I could never think of much to say when we were involved in something meaningful. At this point, my mother appeared in her best coat. She was plainly coming with us. In his eyes, I saw the familiar look of a man thwarted. We went to hospital in my car and his pyjamas were showing from the start.

He must have hated the antiseptic smell. He must have loathed it with all his being. He was a man who, when he felt ill, would say, 'Just go down to Emeric's and get me a good bottle.' Emeric was the chemist. A good bottle was better than a heart transplant any day. My father walked jauntily as if all was well. Only his hands betrayed him then. They were trembling, not because of his possible condition but because it was there to be discussed and disseminated by strangers. We sat on a wooden bench waiting for a radiologist. A chest X-ray was called for.

'Mr Mather?' said the radiologist, a young chap. My father leapt to his feet as if shot. 'Take your shirt and vest off, leave your trousers on, put your jacket on when you have taken off your shirt and vest.'

'Now then,' said my father who, all his life, repeated anything he considered important several times. 'Take my shirt off and my vest, and then what?'

We went through it all, slowly, and he disappeared into a cubicle still wearing his cap. Some time later, when the queue for X-rays had grown somewhat, there was a call from the radiologist and a bellow from the cubicle:

'Right-ho, Joe!'

I pulled aside his curtain and he had done as he was asked, but still wore his cap. When he saw the curtain move, he came out like a whippet and disappeared into the nearest room, a store cupboard of some kind, entirely without lighting, with me in pursuit. The radiologist, startled, herded him into the proper department and there was a long wait. Eventually, my father returned looking quite bright, but the radiologist seemed off colour.

'He said to me,' said my father, ' "What age are you?" "Go on," I said, "guess." '

Such other horrors as had afflicted the National Health Service in the shape of the radiologist remained obscure, but I could imagine:

'Would you stand there, Mr Mather, and keep quite still.'

'Now you want me to stand here, is it?'

'Yes, stand there.'

'And keep still?'

'Yes.'

'Here, is it, then?'

I could forecast the form of conversation almost precisely since I had gone through many such conversations.

We took my father to his ward and he eventually appeared from behind a screen in blue-striped pyjamas. Two nurses were making up a bed. He began to climb into it. 'What are you doing?' asked one nurse. 'Getting into bed,' said my father. 'Well, if you want to,' she said. 'But you are only here for observation.'

He had not anticipated that. He stood there uncertainly, staring at his bed mates. One to the left had a huge beard and a hernia. 'I know you,' said the beard, staring at my father. 'Is it Ben?' I was about to leap in and say, 'Ben is his brother,' but it was as well not to do such things. My father had his own way of dealing with people, and staring at them without comment was sometimes part of the ritual.

'Grand fellow, Ben,' said the beard. 'Knew him well.' My father remained mute. Eventually, he said, 'I'll have a good talk when they've gone.' My father's good talks could last for days. The chap with the beard, I noted, was incapable of movement. Escape was denied him. When I got my mother outside, I said, 'Did he know the chap with the beard?' 'Of course,' she said. 'We sold him our radio.'

I remembered that radio. It was enormous and full of valves. There was nothing like it on earth. Each week, a tiny textile worker named Fred Stubbins used to tend it for a shilling a time. 'It needs a new F4,' he would say. We never knew what he meant. An F4 would be a valve of some sort, one of those bulbous objects that glowed and burned your hand. In truth, I do not believe the radio needed attention on a weekly basis. Fred liked to come for his shilling and always stayed for supper. We went along with the harmless deception.

It was part of that deception that Fred should add a few wires to the thousand or so that were already inside the set. I had never seen such a jungle. When Fred died, my father looked inside the set and decided that at least half the wires were surplus to his requirements, so he pulled out huge mounds of them, showing little discrimination. The set seemed to improve. And this set, I assume, was the one sold to the beard.

My father was in and out of hospital several times after that, and it all culminated in a two-and-a-half-hour operation on his stomach. The first time I saw him after surgery, he had a coloured fellow as a companion – beard on one side, coloured fellow on the other. 'This chap,' said my father, pointing directly at the coloured man, 'is not so bad, you know. Oh, no. Not a bad chap at all. He's a nice sort of chap. He's ...' and here he tapped his own face with the first finger of his right hand. 'You know, he's ...' 'I know,' I said hurriedly. 'How are you?'

My father was not to be put off. 'He's a serious case, you know,' he said loudly. 'Got a lot wrong with him.' He then pointed in turn to each of the people in the ward describing their ailments. He implied that they were, for the most part, 'soft' – moaning away all night long, not able to take a bit of pain like they should; probably poor humpers, the sort Vincent should avoid.

'That one,' he said, pointing, arm fully outstretched, 'is ninety, face like a little orange. He had all his clothes pushed back and his little knees up shouting, "Nurse, nurse." "What's up?" I said to him, and he wanted his pot. "Just a minute," I said, and I went for it, but it was too late. I was just getting his little tassel undone when it happened and I didn't get his pot under him. "Good lord in heavens," I said. "Wheel him out." These others didn't like it, you know. They were having their dinner.'

Later, his opinion of the coloured bedfellow had changed. 'Yon mon,' he said, tapping his own face with one finger again, ' – the one who's, you know? He throws his arms about when he's asleep. Knocked my bottle off this radiator. Knocked my glass, half full, across my bed. When the nurse came, I said, "It was him, not me, threshing about." '

I gather my father's attitude might have brushed off. Someone had asked the coloured man whether he could sign his name on a document before leaving, and he had pointed out that he could not only sign but speak several languages. 'No offence meant nor intended,' I can hear them saying ...

At one stage, my father was on the opposite side of the ward, bedded next to a young chap with 'Love' tattooed across his knuckles. My father did not like that. Arm rigid, he pointed to this man and complained, 'Love – tattooed – God bless my life ...' Then, pointing to someone else. 'And him – he's only had waterworks and he's tottering about half dead. I've no time for 'em.' If I did not stare in the direction he pointed, he would continue to point and his voice would grow louder: 'Look, look where I'm pointing.' These were not relaxed occasions. When he had his operation the thing that delighted him was that he did not moan at all. 'You can ask anybody in this ward,' he said, 'whether I moaned or not, and they'll tell you. Now this fellow next to me' – pointing at a new companion – 'he's been badly crushed at work. He's in a bad way, yon mon. And him across, they've had three doctors to him all night. Road accident.'

The nurses had indicated, by phone, that the old man was not so good himself. 'If you want to know more,' they said, 'have a word with the doctor.'

He had terminal cancer, but he looked as if he were ready for a ten-mile walk. He had nothing but water for a week. Already he was washing himself and making his own toilet arrangements. 'I've missed a lot of work,' he said, and I had visions of Vincent surrounded by a thousand heavy boxes. But he added, 'I should have been up at your place seeing to your fences.'

My mother seemed to have avoided the entire sequence of events between his first arriving and the operation. She said, 'They haven't operated on his chest, you know. It's his stomach.' I said, I knew that. The chest X-ray was routine. 'Well,' she said, 'I was sure it was his chest because he had spots on his back, like moles. He said to me one day, "What are these things on my back? Scratch them off, will you?" But I wasn't going to scratch them off. He'd have bled.'

He said he had never worried about things like that. He had never worried about going into hospital. God bless his life, there was nothing to going into hospital. Get it over, that was his motto. Nobody had cause to worry about him. Not at all. He'd be back walking ten miles before ten in a morning, before others like him had their breakfasts, so there was not a single thing to worry about.

But if anything should happen, I knew where his keys were, and his papers were all together in the safe upstairs.

He lasted for some time and what the illness took away was his strength and his dignity. They were the two things in life he had been most proud of.

Lancashire people of our generation were obsessed by the threat of tuberculosis – then a fatal disease – which was common among cotton workers, and it was thought that lack of food might have caused it. Consequently, children were stuffed with food, mostly starches and fats (to grease the lungs) as a preventative. Our ailments were not understood by doctors or ourselves.

Jim Partington, author, writing in 1971 at the age of sixty-three
(The Two-up and Two-downer, Fabians, Worsley, Manchester)

6

THE TACKLER LIVES: A RIPPING YARN

*I*T WOULD BE WRONG TO ASSUME that the tackler is dead. He is alive, and well, and thriving in other forms. He walks the streets now as a plumber, a doctor, a grocer, a dentist. But the re-birth has not obscured his original character.

I have a friend, a professional man both well-intentioned and well-regarded, and he lives in a dream home. A dream home is a newspaper term for any home at all containing reasonably balanced and optimistic people. Anything over four bedrooms is a mansion in a stockbroker belt. But this is by the way ...

This friend's dream home is well-equipped and compact.

His family having matured and moved upwards and onwards, he applied himself to the task of making one small room into a guest room. He needed paint for the doors, a couch that would turn into a bed, a new carpet and some three-core flex for a new plug. Well, then, what could be simpler?

He chose the carpet and had the man come to measure up (carpet-laying, he decided, was beyond his capacity). He gave the door several coats of white paint and each time was not satisfied. Tricks of shadow and light as the door drifted to and fro on its hinges led him to believe that the original colour was showing through.

This unhinged him. He became obsessed by the shadows. It also unhinged the door. He removed it for better observation. Then he found he could not replace it, and had to send for A Man. This Man duly came and charged £30 for executing the task.

This meant that the door was no longer unhinged, but my friend still was – by this charge, which he (and I for that matter) considered preposterous. He took himself to a high-street store to buy flex. He knew precisely where to look, having bought flex there before. Upstairs. An assistant Upstairs said Downstairs and the assistant Down-stairs said they had stopped selling flex.

Eyes bloodshot from the visions of shadows on white doors, £30 charges for door hanging, and the unavailability of flex, he swept from the store in low dudgeon (it would have been high dudgeon had he not lived in a bungalow), and in doing so caught his jacket on a protruding bit of the store's metal. The jacket ripped. The jacket was expensive. He asked to see the manager and pointed out the rip. The manager was apologetic. He said he had noted the jacket earlier and was impressed, at that time, by its quality. All would be made well.

'I do not want any invisible repairs,' said my friend, 'because this is an expensive jacket and it will show.'

The manager saw no contradiction in this statement. He said my friend would hear from the insurance company within days.

My friend found flex, returned home, and occupied himself with the task of fitting the plug. Having read about do-it-yourself men who are blown to perdition by electricity, he turned it off at the meter, and went about his task. His burglar alarm went off. He knelt there, with the screwdriver, wondering whether he was hearing aright. Could it be someone else's?

He switched off the alarm, went back to the task, touched his plug with the screwdriver, and the alarm went off again. It is well known that alarms have no effect whatsoever on passers-by, but they have a terrible effect on their owners and neighbours. Aware of this terrible effect, he eventually managed to keep the alarm at bay while installing a three-pin plug. As a master craftsman, he was careful to conceal the wire in the tiny gap between skirting boards and floorboards.

He and his wife then tested that the paint was thoroughly dry on the newly-hung, quadruply-painted door, and carefully slid the new couch-bed on its side towards its appointed place. There was the unmistakable sound of tearing. It was a similar sound to that he had heard in the do-it-yourself store.

The new couch-bed was mortally wounded – ripped by a screw which the carpet man had left protruding from the metal implement that joins carpets together between door jambs.

The carpet man was duly informed, in fairly straightforward terms, about his responsibilities in the matter, and my friend was, in turn, informed by the carpet man that an upholsterer would be sent.

So from one small task emerged a whole flowering of events: a disconsolate, but richer, door-hanger, a chastened store manager, a pained carpet fitter, a happy upholsterer, a couple of dozen twitchy neighbours alarmed by an alarm, and a couple in a dream home wondering where the next stab of fate was coming from.

It came fairly quickly as it happens. My diligent friend put a nail through a water pipe beneath the floorboards. He phoned me to tell me so. I told him he needed one of those implements that detects pipes before you apply nails. He did not seem unduly grateful for the advice.

I know that feeling. It is the reason I am no longer a do-it-yourself man. If my friend had accidentally nailed his father-in-law's shoe to a plank, as I did during my early years of marriage, he would have been a wiser, and possibly richer, man thereafter.

The old tacklers need not have condemned themselves overmuch for their discrepancies.

A weaver living next to a mill was invariably late for work while one who lived a mile away was always on time. The tackler noted this and put it to the culprit.

'Look here,' he said, 'how is it you can't get here on time when another does and travels so far?'

'That's simple,' said the weaver. 'If he gets up late he can run. If I get up late, I've no choice.'

A Lancashire husband and wife on a London tube train.

Wife: 'I do feel sick.'

Husband: 'Well, don't be sick here. According to that notice it costs forty shillings just to spit.'

Tackler: 'Now, what's bothering you?'

Weaver: 'They're all talking about me.'

'Oh, and what are they saying?'

'They say I'm having a baby.'

'Well, what are you bothered about? They can't talk it so.'

'Ah, but that's just it. They have done.'

A weaver applied to a tackler for a job and received the following reply: 'I have a man here who hasn't come yet. If he doesn't turn up by eight o'clock I'll send him home and you can have his place.'

(Believed true.)

A weaver complained that her shuttle kept flying out and hitting the same brick in the wall, so a tackler removed the brick.

After complaints about the amount of toilet paper being used, a tackler checked the lavatory after each weaver had used it. He had numbered the entire roll in pencil the night before.

A tackler who bought a motor-bike was asked, weeks later, how it was running.
    'It's grand,' he said, 'only I can't go out when it's dark.'
    'Why's that?'
    'I've been in every shop in town and not one sells red lamp oil.'

During a Wakes [annual holiday] week when everyone else had gone away, a tackler was seen wheeling an empty barrow. 'What are you doing with that?' someone asked.
    'Well,' said the tackler, 't'missus has gone to Morecambe, my dog's gone sick, t'lad spends all his time in bed, and a fellow feels so daft walking about by himself.'

Two out-of-work tacklers found themselves in the mining area around Wigan. One decided to ask for employment.
    'Are you a miner?' asked the manager.
    'No,' replied the tackler.
    'Pity,' said the manager. 'I could have found you a place.'
    The tackler told his friend what had happened.
    'You're daft,' said the friend. 'All you had to do was tell him you'd done a bit of pit work.'
    The second tackler then went to the pit office and asked for a job.
    'Have you any experience?' said the manager.
    'I've done a bit,' said the tackler.
    'And what kind of lamps have you been used to?'
    'Well, to be truthful, I've never been on t'night shift.'

A tackler left his mill to become manager at another and weavers clubbed together to buy him a watch. Later, one of the weavers was employed at the same mill as the tackler once more. One morning, she arrived late to be met by the manager. 'Do you see that?' said the manager, tapping the face of his watch. 'I should hope so,' said the weaver. 'I helped buy it.'

A tackler asked an engineer to cut two inches from each end of a plain shaft he needed for a loom. The engineer said he would cut four inches from one end. 'You mustn't do that,' said the tackler. 'It would be too short.'

A mill manager asked a tackler to report on the state of gas mantles supplying light to the weaving shed.

'Every one of 'em needs renewing,' reported the tackler.

'That seems unlikely,' said the manager. 'What makes you think that?'

'I felt at t'lot and they were all soft.'

A tackler walking in the countryside asked a farmer how his crop was faring. 'Not so bad so far as I can see,' said the farmer, 'but of course, I don't know what it's like in t'middle of t'field and I don't want to walk over it and spoil it.'

'That's not a problem,' said the tackler. 'Me and my friend can carry you.'

A tackler who bought a hen house asked two friends to help him shift it two miles to his own plot of land. The helpers had to take frequent rests and they realised, eventually, that the owner was no-where to be seen.

'That's funny,' said one, 'he's vanished altogether.'

'Nay, I haven't' said the owner from inside the hen house. 'I'm in here carrying t'perches.'

A tackler to whom a mill worker kept going, first for one thing, then another, quoted, 'I need thee every hour.'

She replied, 'Abide by me.'

'My sister went to her tackler, told him her shuttle kept flying out, and he said, "Cut its bloody wings off."'

A mill owner introducing his son to the business put him to work with a tackler for guidance. Some time later, he sent for the tackler and said, 'Well now, and how is that son of mine getting along?'

'Well,' said the tackler, 'I'm sorry to have to tell you this, but he'll never be up to much. I've taught him all I know and he knows nowt yet.'

A farmer wishing to get a cow on top of a building covered in grass called a tackler for advice. The tackler suggested a pulley. They were winding the animal up when a stranger asked what they were doing. They told him.

'Wouldn't it be better,' he said, 'to cut the grass and bring it down to the cow?'

The tackler thought for a while, then said to the farmer, 'You see what book learnin' does for you?'

(True.)

We had a tackler who, when a shuttle flew out, would follow the trail of weft from loom to shuttle. We wrapped the weft twice round a pillar in the shed, threw the shuttle under a loom, then watched his face as he tried to figure it out. Years later, overlookers, by then including myself, were on a bench in the weft cellar when the boss arrived with a visitor and said, 'They are the best-paid people in the factory.'

'Why don't you get them working?' asked the visitor.

'Nay, lad,' said the boss. 'If I get them up they'll only start cutting up leather and that costs two shillings a piece.'

C. B. Fawcett, Nelson.

A tackler walked home along a canal towpath and came across a workmate, a fellow tackler, on hands and knees scooping water from the canal with the bottom part of his enamel brew tin.

'What are you doing, Fred?'

'I dropped my wages in t'canal and I'm scooping t'watter out to get 'em back.'

'You'll never manage,' said the tackler. 'Give us t'lid and I'll help you.'

A newly-wed tackler was given tenancy of a mill house and the manager asked him to let him know if there was anything he needed. 'Well,' said the young man, 'there's no lock on t'little back door of th'outside closet – the one for emptying t'tub.'

'Jack,' said the manager, 'I've looked after these houses for fifteen years and we've never had a tub o'muck pinched yet.'

More than fifty years ago, I was a warehouse boy at Weaver's Mill, Brierfield. At times, we were pestered by mice, so we bought a cat. A tackler cut a hole in the bottom of a door so that the cat could go in and out when the mill was closed. When the cat had kittens, he cut a smaller hole next to the big one for them all to go in and out.

Jack Dee, Padiham.

Two weavers met.

'Aren't you working?' asked one.

'No,' replied the other. 'I told my husband that t'tackler winked at me and he said, "You go there no more." It's grand being at home.'

Her friend decided to try something similar. 'Hey, Joe,' she said to her husband, 't'tackler winked at me today.'

'You wink right back,' said her husband. 'He might give you another loom to run.'

A tackler and his wife visited friends who had bought a gas fire, which they much admired. 'Did you get a gas fire?' asked the friends weeks later.

'I did and all,' said the tackler, 'and it's doing champion. We lit it when we got it and it hasn't gone out since.'

Early morning. Tackler preparing fire, wife in bed.

Tackler: 'Where are t'matches, love?'

'There aren't any.'

'Never mind, then, I'll light a candle.'

A tackler who had just bought a new house was asked by a merchant whether he needed any coal.

'Ee, no, lad,' he said. 'I won't ever be needing any. There's hot and cold water in all my taps.'

A tackler sat at a bench writing a letter.

'What are you doing?' asked a friend.

'I'm writing to one of them clothing catalogues for a frock for t'wife. I've written, "Please find enclosed photographs of my wife. Send me a red dress wattle fit her."'

Said his friend, 'It's not wattle, you clown, it's ussle.'

A doctor advised a tackler to give his sick wife sufficient medicine to cover a sixpence. Next day, the doctor said, 'Is she any better?'

'Not much,' replied the tackler.

'Did you give her the medicine?'

'Aye, I did, but I didn't have a sixpence so I gave it to her on five pennies and two halfpennies.'

A doctor treating the head of the house for constipation did not appear to be making headway. He increased the dose of medicine so that eventually there was enough 'to shift a horse'. As he walked towards the house one day, he saw his patient's son walking down the other side of the road. 'Has your father had a motion yet?' he shouted.

'Aye, he has, doctor,' replied the lad. 'Once afore he died and twice after.'

(True.)

Two tacklers talking about a new toilet one had installed at home.

'It's all right, but it is not as good as the old one. It's so cold to sit on.'

'Didn't you have a wooden oval seat supplied with it?'

'Hell, yes, but I thought that was a picture frame. I've got t'wife's picture hung up in it.'

A tackler walked a couple of miles to see a friend, also a tackler.

'Harry,' he said, 'can I borrow your ladder?'

'Aye,' said Harry. 'What do you want it for?'

'Wife wants me to cut a V shape in her clothes prop.'

'Nay,' said Harry, 'it's fellows like you gets tacklers a bad name. Why don't you rear t'prop up against t'bedroom window?'

A tackler who wanted to cut a dash on his motor-bike sought a cap, but when he had inspected all the styles available at the outfitter's he found that none was suitable.

'I can't understand this,' said the assistant. 'We have every style here that you could get in t'whole of Manchester. What are you particularly looking for?'

'Well,' said the tackler, 'I've got a motor-bike, you see, and all these caps have nebs at t'front. I want a cap with a neb at t'back.'

A tackler keeping hens and living by a railway line kept losing the odd one as it was hit by a train, so he asked the stationmaster for a timetable.

'You know t'times of trains well enough,' said the stationmaster. 'Why do you want a timetable?'

'To pin on t'hen cabin,' said the tackler, 'as a reminder.'

A river overflowed and water flooded houses around a mill. As householders went to work with bucket and mop, a tackler just smoked his pipe and looked on.

'Are you not going to shift your water?' asked a neighbour.

'Nay,' said the tackler, 'I've more sense. All I have to do is wait for t'tide to go out.'

Two mill workers who crossed a field rather than go a longer journey by road were met by a farmer at the other side. 'What do you think you are doing?' said the farmer. 'Can't you see there's no road?'

'Correct,' said one of the two. 'There doesn't seem to be much of a road, but we'll make do with it.'

A tackler starting work in a new town was offered a bed provided he shared the room with a coloured man. He agreed and went to sleep. The coloured man, returning to find what appeared to be an interloper, blacked the tackler's face with soot. The tackler, running to work next morning, saw his face reflected in the glass of a shop front. 'Good heavens,' he thought, 'she's wakened t'wrong fellow.'

A parson out walking, carrying his Bible, wrapped it in his red and white spotted handkerchief when rain came down. Two men were working on a hole in the road, one above and one below ground. The one above was cursing.

'My man,' said the parson, displeased, 'do you not know God?'

The workman observed the parson and his bundle and shouted to his friend, 'Hey, Bill, do you know God? There's a fellow here with his dinner.'

A retired tackler talking about driving in 1925: 'Of course, there were no modern cars in those days.'

Old-style East Lancashire local politician making an election speech: 'I want you all to think of me as a public convenience and use me whenever possible.'

Mechanic, to doctor stranded on moors with his Ford Popular: 'No wonder it won't go. This battery is flat.'

'Oh,' said the doctor, 'what shape should it be?'

Police officer attempting to keep a check on an East Lancastrian who had been in a little trouble with the law: 'Where are you working now, Harry?'

'Here and theer.'

'Oh, and where's that?'

'Up and down.' The police officer looked puzzled.

'Tha knows – round about,' said the man, looking helpful.

'And what kind of thing are you doing?'

'This and that ...'

A girl admired a pair of stirrups mounted on a pub wall and called her boyfriend's attention to them.

'I gave them to t'landlord,' said the boyfriend.

Girl (sharply, not believing him): 'You what?'

'I said I know who gave them to him.'

Girlfriend (less interested now): 'Oh, who?'

'I did.'

'Your dog's just bitten me.'

'It couldn't have done. It has no teeth.'

'It's given me a dam'd good suck, then.'

Frank Randle.

Helmshore has been agog this week with the story of the political conversion of a pig. In the neighbourhood there lives a clogger of well-known and pronounced political convictions. Last municipal election, he avowed that all his family were Tory to the core, but he would not speak definitely about the politics of the pig he kept. The animal is kept in a sty situated near Mr Rawstron Whitaker's works and, perhaps fearing that the grunter would also imbibe beliefs of blue, someone on Wednesday night interviewed it with a pot of paint and brush. When the owner went to give piggy its breakfast on Thursday morning, he found it had been embellished all over with red paint, and for a time wondered if the jubilations of the previous night (to celebrate a Conservative victory in Helmshore ward) had left their impression on his mind. But there was no mistake; there was the radical-hued pig. He set to work scrubbing it with soda and hot water with the hope of accomplishing a reconversion, but when he found his scrubbing brought off more skin than paint, he desisted. Housewives are looking for some good Liberal bacon.

Haslingden Guardian, *4 November 1893.*

'I spy something beginning wi' T.'

'Table?'

'No.'

'Trifle?'

'No.'

'Teapot?'

'No.'

'What, then?'

'T'oven door.'

A mill clerk bought a new bowler and hung it on a peg outside his office door. The name of the hatter was printed on an inside band. Weavers took it back to the shop and exchanged it for an identical, but larger, hat. The clerk, leaving work, wore the hat over his ears, but said nothing. That night, he packed the inside band with tissue paper, and when he arrived at work next morning, the hat fitted well enough once more. Again, the weavers took it back to the shop and exchanged it for the original bowler, which they stuffed with the tissue paper. The clerk, donning the hat after work, then found that it perched on top of his head. He said nothing. But next morning there was a phone call from his wife: 'My husband will not be coming to work today. He says there's something wrong with his head.'

'Remember, the hardest way in life is always the most difficult.' There were murmurs of, 'Hear, hear.'

Extract from a speech by an East Lancashire councillor.

Mayor at council meeting: 'Them houses aren't fit for human consumption.'

A councillor who objected to the council buying new horses to haul refuse carts proposed that, in future, they should buy second-hand horses.

A former mayor: 'When I were a lad at skoo, t'teacher said to me, "What do you want to be when you grow up?" an' I said, "Please, miss, mur of Accrington."'

'And did you know, God, that they've put up a new lamp post in Avenue Parade?'

Child's prayer, Accrington.

A town clerk with a sense of humour wrote a speech for his mayor during the Second World War. Throughout, he referred to incendiary bombs as 'insanitary bombs'.

Haslingden had a town clerk named Bull. A child at Helmshore wrote in an essay about mayor-making: 'The procession was led by Mr Clerk, the Town Bull.'

Princess Margaret, accompanied by elected representatives of the people, had the following conversation with their leader:
'Mind these steps, ma'am.'
'Why, has someone fallen down them?'
'Nay, but we don't want thee to be t'fost.'

A councillor who, at one meeting, voted for a £100,000 public works scheme later voted against it. He was asked why. 'Well,' he said, 'there's nowt theer you couldn't do wi' two good Irish labourers and a barrow.'

7

ALL ABOARD THE
GRAVY TRAIN

A MUCH-ADMIRED EATER in Lancashire drank on a similar scale and deserved credit on both counts. He had much in common with the bottomless pit. Four or five Amontillados at the premises of the Messrs Yates would be followed by several pints of ale, and at half time (around 9 p.m. on a Saturday night) he would take, for purposes of resuscitation, a pound of tripe before moving on to several more pints of ale. Sometimes, towards the end, that ritualistic time of night when the doors were closing and the lads were shredding each other on the boulevard, he sweated a little, but he never swayed, which is just as well. He was a rotund person. Had he ever fallen on a hill, he would have rolled for miles.

On Friday nights, greens, in the form of radishes, lettuces, spring onions and so forth, floated in his bath, which was half filled with water, and they covered its surface to a depth of six inches or so. He ate them all, on his own, over a weekend. One imagines that in hard times, he would have cropped a small field.

I accompanied him on some of his expeditions, a pale shadow attempting to keep pace with this remarkable and portly substance, and not really fit company for someone as accomplished as him. He had done the grand tour of Europe in his early manhood, and by some curious alchemy, this propelled him towards a lifetime of betting, eating, drinking, and story-telling. I, for one, am grateful because he was part of my education.

He used to say that no-one knew what betting was until they had spent time in the Adelphi Hotel in Liverpool waiting for the New York cotton spot prices to come in. I seem to recall some dispute at that hotel involving how much tripe my friend could eat. Some might well have suggested that he could speak rather more than he could eat. The argument became heated, so everyone involved went in dark of night to a tripe shop and roused the proprietor. There was a weigh-in before the devouring. At any rate, my friend proved whatever point he was choosing to make.

We were in a pub together once when some stranger arrived who seemed to be the most travelled man in the world. My friend latched on to him and they had an animated, if one-sided conversation. It took in most of the capitals of Europe together with their most notable hotels, streets, chefs, claims to fame and so on. My friend not only knew each one mentioned, but added bits and pieces of his own information, all of it of an intimate nature. The much-travelled man, who remained virtually wordless throughout, eventually left, and as he disappeared beyond the pub door, my friend shook his head admiringly and said, 'What a character!'

A national newspaper once published a picture of a horse race in progress during a violent and sudden rainstorm, and there they were streaking about in the mud with only one spectator at the rails. It was my rotund friend, of course, recognisable immediately by his shape and general air of absorbed attention. He was some sort of legend, but by no means the greatest legend, and I reckon I saw the best of him before he vanished, quite inexplicably, arriving eventually at Barrow-in-Furness, that drip on the nose of Britain dedicated to the building of ships in monotonous isolation.

His reputation lived on in East Lancashire, and in Blackburn and Darwen (where he made his home for much of his time) in particular. The great eating days had gone in Darwen when I went to re-awaken memories in the early 'seventies, and he was then the echo rather than the substance. The man who inspired real awe was named Cecil. I had not previously met Cecil though I had, of course, heard of his great devourings. He was serving at his market stall. There were no rivals within reach or sight but now, he said, he was 'troubled with my stomach.' I am not surprised. His stomach had been troubled by Cecil for long enough.

He was seventy-nine, he said, and saw no reason to recall the days when, with a bite and a gulp, he built his massive reputation. So we stood there, awkwardly, Cecil declaring, perhaps out of modesty, that he would say nothing, a mutual friend and myself prodding gently; and finally, he relented.

'I could eat a hundred oranges as fast as anybody could quarter them with a blade,' he said. I knew that. Everyone within fifty miles knew it. In the last gasps of their lives, Darwen people still held the vision of a hundred oranges on a bar top. I looked suitably surprised, however, to encourage him. An old woman who fingered his lettuces and declared them not up to standard was eyed with disdain by the great devourer and dismissed as an irrelevance. Cecil acknowledged, in full, the magnificence of his stomach and listed its achievements.

'– a hundred oranges and then I'd go home and have a meal.'

'He did,' my companion confirmed. 'I know that.'

Then he added, 'His ripping teeth have gone. He used to rip quarter oranges out of the peel with one movement.'

Someone once challenged Cecil that he would eat a hundred oranges faster, but he never turned up.

'Ten pounds of tripe in ten minutes,' said Cecil. 'I'd eat that.'

'That's a good-sized bucketful,' said my guide, 'but of course, it was seasoned to his palate.'

'– and one day,' said Cecil, 'I went to market and it was raining so I called in a pub and began to play darts. I was drinking stout and got interested in the game, and eventually I said, "I'll just have another."'

'No, you won't,' said the landlord.

'Why?' asked Cecil. 'Have I spoken out of turn?'

'No,' said the landlord. 'There isn't any. You've gone through six dozen bottles. I know, because I was carrying them upstairs when you came in.'

'And that,' said my guide later – because we were hushed with respect at the time – 'was non-competitive, you understand.'

'I used to bet £2,' said Cecil, 'plus the cost of the food or drink.'

The woman at the tripe stall across from Cecil's, overhearing all this, said she would not mind someone having a go at her stock, someone like Cecil. Cecil waved his acknowledgement: it was reminiscent of the queen's royal gestures as she proceeds through throngs of her subjects.

'I once saw a chap on a market,' he said, 'and he had a lot of pies left on his stall. I asked him, "Have you had a good day?" and he said, "No – look at all these." I said, "There's nowt there. I could eat the lot."' He did, too, for a £2 bet. Cecil saw the stallholder again some time later and it was the start of a day, the stall high with pies. 'Do you want to double up?' asked Cecil. 'Four pounds and I'll eat the lot?'

'Not likely,' said the trader. 'You'd eat t'dam'd stall, you would.' Cecil said that in the old days he had a big stalk of bananas and he would take off a bundle, perhaps eighteen at a time, and eat them between serving customers.

We left the old man eyeing his own mountain of greenery, but the champion's jaws were stilled, the nostrils unflared, the ripping teeth blunted and discarded, the gastric juices in disarray: before us had stood the only man in living memory thereabouts who could eat his own height in meat pies.

'There have been some great bets in these parts,' said my guide, 'but you know the one bet no eater will take?'

I said I did, for my education had not been entirely neglected: a pigeon a day for a month.

'That's it,' said my guide. 'I know people who would eat a couple of dozen at a go without trouble, but no-one would eat one a day for a month. Something to do with a pigeon not digesting inside twenty-four hours.'

I said we had better keep that one to ourselves. There's a fortune in knowledge like that if you use it the right way.

A textile worker was going to brew up, so she asked a spinner for his tea and sugar. The spinner replied, 'T'tea's coffee.' She asked him for his jug. He said 'T'jug's a can.'

When she returned with the coffee, he saw that grains were floating on the surface.

'What's this?' he said.

'Hot water was cold,' she replied.

A tackler alone in a Devon pub. A barmaid puts a pint in front of him.

'What's that?' he asks.

'It's a pint from that fellow at the other end, the one with a moustache. He says he was at school with you.'

'Nay, best take it back. There was nobody in our class wi' a moustache.'

'Ee, come here and I'll stab thee wi' my pickle tooth.'

Frank Randle.

During the depression years of the 'thirties two out-of-work Lancastrians in need of a pint went to their local pub, ordered two half-pints of beer, and said to the landlord, 'We were just having an argument. How many pints in a quart?'

'Two,' said the landlord.

Later, when the landlord was busy elsewhere, they said to the barmaid, 'Two pints, love; they're paid on by the landlord.'

'Are you sure?' she said.

'Oh, aye,' replied one, then – 'Landlord, you did say two pints didn't you?'

'That's right,' said the landlord.

(True)

Deception carried out in Lancashire pubs long ago. A stranger enters when trade is busy and begins to do simple tricks – pulling playing cards from people's pockets, and so on. After a while, he says to the landlord, 'Give me one of your pound notes and I will make it reappear in your till. And make a note of the number.'

The landlord complies, urged on by his customers. Further tricks are performed, then the stranger says, 'Landlord – the pound is back in your till.'

Sure enough, the pound is there. Everyone applauds. The stranger disappears. The landlord has been deprived of his money. How? The conjuror has handed the pound note to an accomplice, who has been sitting anonymously with other customers. The accomplice has bought a drink from the other side of the bar using the landlord's pound note and receiving the change.

A tackler went to Australia, made a fortune, came back, walked down the main street of his home town, did not recognise a thing, then found a faulty neon sign on a pub which read 'Billards', when it should have read 'Billiards'. He went inside and said, 'Give me a pint of that billards.' The barman thought, 'I've got a right one here' and served him a pint of washing up water to teach him a lesson. The tackler took a good gulp, thought a bit, took another gulp, then said, 'If I hadn't been a great billards drinker from way back, I'd have said that was washing up water. But' – taking another swig – 'it's billards.'

City gent enters pub on Lancashire moors, sits next to tackler and, when the barmaid arrives, says, 'Tickle your arse with a feather.'

'You what?' she asks sharply.

'Particularly nasty weather,' he said.

'Oh,' she replies.

'Hey,' says the tackler, 'what did you say to that lass?'

The city gent explained.

'Ee,' says the tackler, 'that's a good 'un. I'll try that at t'Red Lion.'

He exited soon afterwards so as not to forget the words, burst into the Red Lion, and cried 'Hey!' to a barmaid.

'What?' she replied.

'I'd like to see your bum.'

'I beg your pardon!' she said, and he replied, 'It's picklin' down outside.'

A tackler noted for his fondness for chewing tobacco approached a colleague at the mill and said, 'Hey, Fred, have you a mouthful of 'bacca?'

'No,' said Fred.

'I've nobbut half an ounce.'

A tackler limped as he went about his work. 'What's up?' said a friend.

'Neuritis. It's in my leg.'

'Have you tried going teetotal for it?'

'Well, to be honest, I've thowt about it, but I can't make up my mind whether to be without ale or without neuritis.'

When a barrel of beer was sent back by a pub as being unfit for sale, the brewery manager offered it to the lads in the yard. Days later, he was walking across the yard when he spotted the foreman. 'Well, Jack,' he said, 'did you get that barrel of ale I sent you?'

'Aye, we did.'

'And how was it?'

'Just right.'

'Nay, Jack, it couldn't have been just right. T'pub had sent it back.'

'Aye,' said Jack, 'I know that. But if it had been any better we wouldn't have got it and if it had been any worse we couldn't have supped it, so it were just right.'

Two tacklers going home from work on a hot day.

First tackler: 'By gum, it's warm. I think I'll call for a gill of beer.'

Second tackler: 'Aye, and if it's like this next week, I'll have one, too.'

A tackler and an Irishman became friends. The Irishman's weakness was drink. He was a firebeater at a mill and because he did not arrive on time on a Monday, after his excesses of the weekend, he was fired. The tackler later found his friend standing outside the Red Lion. 'Lend me a shilling, John,' said the Irishman.

'I will,' said the tackler, 'but don't you think you would be better off outside the pub rather than in it? After all, drink is what got you sacked.'

'All I want,' said the Irishman, 'is one drink and then I'll be finished with it for good. Next time you find me waitin' outside the Red Lion, I'll be in Canada.'

A Lancastrian earned a few drinks and fewer coppers by playing his violin in pubs. On a dark night, his wife lit a small candle and put it in the window so that he could be guided towards it as he walked across the fields. He burst into the house crying, 'Here am I, working my fingers to t'bone, and my house a blaze o'light.'

A tackler about to be married went to a jeweller's and asked to see wedding rings.

'Eighteen carat?' said the jeweller.

'No,' said the tackler, 'I'm chewing tobacco. What's it got to do with thee?'

8

THE MONUMENTAL PUDDING

*T*HE BLACK PUDDING is a Lancashire monument to the extent that it could almost form part of someone's crest. All those bloodied hands on crests were probably reaching for black puddings when they were lopped off. Among the great pudding-makers of Britain, the Thornleys of Chorley, quoting four generations of quality, have stood proud with their craft. The Thornley pudding, originated by grand-father Thornley – no preservatives, no colouring, no artificial flavours – contains barley, oatmeal, herbs, spices, pigs' blood, wheat flour, fresh onions, salt and pepper and pure pork fat. It looks plump, prosperous and rather like polished coal.

Jack Thornley became one of the great contest winners of our time, and a Knight of the Confrerie des Chevaliers du Goute Boudin (black pudding tasters). As a knight he was supposed to eat one pudding a day for life. He reckoned, when I saw him before his retirement, that four times a week was enough.

Once, Thornleys made puddings in a huge dish. Later, they were making fifteen tons a week. 'It makes you wonder where they all go,' Jack said, although he must have had a reasonable idea. His cups and medals became legion. He first won the English championship in Mortagne-au-Perche, in Normandy (a European centre for such things) at the beginning of the 'seventies.

Each year, hundreds of pork butchers and black pudding makers gathered from all over Europe in this tiny French village to be judged by a panel of professional charcutiers in search of the best black pudding in the world, and Jack was a notable contributor. He enjoyed the three-day festivals with their thousands of contestants and visitors, and viewed with a professional eye the long trestle tables laid out with each country's black puddings. During the testing, bottles of the finest wines lubricated the task. And on Saturday night, 8 p.m. to 4 a.m., the grand banquet: third course, boudin (black pudding), eaten with apple just before a toast in Calvados, a distilled apple juice.

In 1980, the BBC produced a documentary/comedy play, written by Brian Glover, entitled *Thicker than Water*. It was based largely on Jack Thornley's winning ways and told the story of a Lancashire black pudding maker called Jackson Arnott. It ended with Jackson Arnott's son winning with a canned black pudding. Reality is somewhat different. Jack Thornley used the standard ninety-year-old recipe.

'Sometimes,' he says, 'you would go to so much trouble making the blessed things and for one reason or another they would just not come out right. These days, people eat so many that we cut the fat by machine so that it has an irregular shape. In competition, we cut by hand, making half-inch cubes. The secret is in the seasoning. There is no meat in a black pudding, of course. I tell everybody they are grown underground, like potatoes, which is why we have a farm of eighty acres.' Did anyone believe him? 'Aye, you'd be amazed.'

The question of whether or not he should go into the business – with two brothers he was concerned with shop, farm and factory, all sprouted from a small shop in Chorley in the late 1890s – never arose. From the age of ten or twelve he spent his free time working at the shop or taking pies around pubs. It never occurred to him that there was anything else to do.

Germans are seen as the best pork butchers in the world and invariably win in contests. German noses and palates find the English black pudding not at all comparable to their own. The construction is different.

'The German pudding,' said Jack, 'is a magnificent structure. You know what a mosaic pavement looks like? Well, you've got something like it in ham, tongue, nuts, and mushrooms and the black pudding mixture is the cement around this mosaic. Absolutely out of this world. How can you judge that against an English pudding? It is different altogether.'

French puddings are different, too. 'German and French do not like the English pudding – neither the flavour nor the herbs we use. And they are the people doing the judging, so we are on a hiding to nothing.'

The Thornleys listed the best alternative ways of serving black pudding, and here they are:

1. Simmer in hot water for ten minutes.
2. Slice in half and fry.

3. Slice in half and grill.

4. Microwave.

5. Dip in batter and deep-fry.

6. Cut up in small pieces and use as meat in hot pot.

7. Serve with mashed potatoes, onion and apple (see recipe).

   (Most of these methods are improved by serving with English mustard.)

8. If eaten cold, slice and make sandwiches, or eat as paté.

Celestial food

Ten ounces sliced black pudding; one pound apples, peeled and sliced; three large potatoes for mashing; one large or two small onions, sliced; two ounces butter; sugar; salt; pepper; nutmeg.

Peel or scrub potatoes, boil until cooked, then mash with a little butter and season to taste. While potatoes are cooking, peel apple and slice, cook with sugar to taste, and a little water to prevent sticking, blend with one ounce of butter. Fry onions in one ounce of butter until soft and keep warm. Line shallow dish with apple purée, arrange slices of black pudding in the dish; pipe mashed potato around dish, place onions over black pudding and put under grill to brown.

Humble pie

One and a half pounds potatoes; quarter pound cooking apples; one pound sliced black pudding in quarter-inch slices (skin removed); one large onion; salt and pepper.

Peel and slice potatoes, apples and onion. Into a casserole dish place slices of black pudding. Cover this with slices of apple, then onion, then potato. Season lightly with salt and pepper. Repeat layers, ending with a layer of potato. Season lightly. Add sufficient water to come half-way up dish. Cover and cook in moderate oven, 375°F, 190°C or gas mark 4–5 for one to one and a half hours. Take off cover and return to oven until top layer of potato is crisp.

A tackler training his dog to catch rabbits tied up the animal at one end of a field and released the rabbit at the other end.

Contributed anonymously, Nelson.

'Go down to t'butcher's and get a sheep's head and tell him to leave t'legs on.'

'Thirties folk joke.

A pub on the moors emptied by the arrival of the breathalyser.

Landlady: 'For all t'good we're doing here we might as well be running a brothel.'

Landlord: 'Nay, if we can't sell ale, we can't sell broth.'

A tackler put two eggs to boil, left the house, got delayed by chatter in the street, and returned realising that the eggs had been in the water for half an hour. He allowed them to cool, then said to his son, 'Take these back to t'shop and tell 'em we wanted duck eggs.'

A Masonic dinner in Blackpool.

Waitress carrying two containers is asking each guest, 'Black or white coffee?'

'Black,' said one guest, then, as she was moving away, added, 'Hey, aren't you going to put any milk in it?'

Same Masonic dinner. Worshipful Master's wife, attempting to make conversation with nearby guest: 'Good meal, isn't it? These forks are nice aren't they?'

'I don't know. I haven't tasted mine yet.'

Party of tacklers in a posher-than-usual restaurant in Blackpool. One drank tea from his saucer, as was his habit.

'Fred,' said his wife, 'drink from your cup.'

'Can't,' said Fred, 'spoon's in t'way.'

A tackler made a bowl of gruel for his sick wife and she complained that he had forgotten to put in a dash of nutmeg. 'Wrong,' he said. 'I put three whole nutmegs in and there's another downstairs if you'd like me to fetch it.'

'Save me a tackler this weekend,' said a customer to a butcher (a tackler being another name for a sheep's head). When Saturday came, he called for the sheep's head and was disappointed at the size of it.

'You're not telling me that's a proper tackler,' he said.

'No,' replied the assistant, 'but it will be when I've taken its brains out.'

'I've plucked t'chicken and stuffed it. All t'wife has to do now is kill it and put it in t'oven.'

Pub scene, Manchester. First drinker: 'Ah, sawdust on the floors. Haven't seen that in years.'

Second drinker: 'That's not sawdust. It's last night's furniture.'

A tackler's wife preparing for Christmas said to her husband, 'Happen you should go to t'shops and get a pound of currants.' She gave him a shilling, then – 'Better I should have some raisins as well. Here's another shilling.' He was away for so long she went in search of him and found him outside the shop window, a shilling in each hand. 'I'm right glad you've come,' he said, 'I don't know which shilling is for currants and which for raisins.'

A tackler's wife brought home butter which tasted not quite right.

'It was all they had,' she said. 'Fellow at t'Co-op said there'll be no more until t'tub is empty.'

'In that case,' said her husband, a Co-op committeeman, 'go back and get another four pounds. Let's have done with it.'

A degrading competition for a wager took place last Friday in a beer shop at Haslingden. One man who rejoices in the name of Jim Balshaw undertook to drink no fewer than ten pints of ale before another man could drink five. And hard though it is to credit, the latter was defeated. We fear that our readers would doubt the veracity were we to state the enormous quantity of beefsteaks, loaves and ale which the prizewinner is said to be able to consume at one time. Therefore, we will not publish the harrowing details. We regret, however, that there should be persons so degraded as to encourage such disgraceful exhibitions as the one alluded to.

Haslingden Guardian, *August 1892.*

James Isherwood, landlord, Blazing Stump, at Bent Gate, near Haslingden undertook at the Black Dog, Haslingden, to eat 20 raw hen eggs together with the shells in 15 minutes. If he won, the company were to pay for the cost and a quart of ale for himself. If he lost, he was to pay for the cost and a gallon of ale for the company. He accomplished the task in seven minutes. The eggs were to have been duck eggs, but none could be produced.

Blackburn Mail, *February 1827.*

A gourmandising feat was undertaken at the Wellington Inn, Has-lingden Grane, on Monday. A volunteer undertook to eat a four-pound pudding composed of one pound flour, one pound suet, a quarter of currants and one and three-quarter pounds of milk and water absorbed in kneading and boiling ... The operator's jaws were brought to a deadlock on eating three-quarters of the pudding.

Haslingden and Rawtenstall Express, *February 1866.*

9

WHATEVER HAPPENED TO THE STOCK POT?

$\mathcal{M}$ ANY A HOUSEWIFE has forgotten all her grandmother knew. She throws away the best parts of her vegetables, lets her lettuce go limp, has never used a stock pot, gives bones to the dog, and wonders what happened to the housekeeping money. That, at any rate, is the theory.

Bill Swift, unique in catering, devoted his life to Lancashire eating. He was probably, before his retirement, the only restaurateur (Hoghton Arms, Withnell, near Chorley) who was also a master butcher. He travelled to Fleetwood for his fish, to Wales for his live lobsters, and once turned up for a holiday in Ibiza with a whole boned Welsh sheep as hand luggage, his family's meat for the week. Here is his philosophy of past and present:

Good food is love, care, planning, feeling. Cookery books are good now, but they too often deal with the most spectacular dishes needing fussy sauces. In the old days, you would never have dreamed of using meat cubes. You started with a stock pot. I cut the bone off the meat before I roast it and then I add onions, ends of celery, carrot ends. The bones have special meaning. Marrow is strength. There is nothing on a beast that needs to be wasted.

So – bones for soups, stocks for cooking, every bit of gravy from the bones going into the stews. And if I get fed up with the stock pot, I throw all the egg shells into it, clarify what little fat there is, and make a clear soup.

People talk about hard times in the 'thirties, but in one sense we lived better. Farmers fed their stock better. Beef was allowed to mature. Now, there is forced feeding and the quality and flavour of meat is not what it was. It is not hung properly. We used to kill and hang the meat for seven to nine days before we even attempted to cut it. Nowadays, it is often on sale within two or three days.

I went into butchering when I was fifteen. There aren't any master butchers around any more. It means being slaughterer, cutter, salesman, making up the smalls – black puddings, potted meats, brawns; being there at 5 or 5.30 a.m. for the slaughtering, ready for the shop opening at 8.30 or 9, the factory workers coming in for breakfast time.

Mondays and Tuesdays they had the offal and nowadays, especially since the meat scares, offal is thought of as rubbish. We regarded it all as good stuff, liver, oxtail, hearts, sweetbreads, kidneys, tongues, feet, tripe, head, suet. Tuesdays, we prepared potted meats and you knew a good one a mile away. We used to make it from our elder briskets. Now, people want steaks: silverside, topside, sirloin. The forequarter beef goes for manufacturing, to the meat pie factories. What the housewife never realises is that when meat is hanging, all the goodness is draining into the cheaper cuts and what is better than a good beef dripping sandwich? A lot of people went to work on that.

Today, you get pressure cookers. People put water on the meat and boil out the goodness. You get a splendid stew if you cut up your onions fine, add them to a little spot of either beef dripping or butter in a hot pan, season the meat chunks, then drop them in. The meat goes to the base of the pan and as you stir it around, the flavour is locked in. If you put water on before the flavour is sealed, you end up with soggy, cottonwool meat, everything in the gravy.

The old family butcher knew the lot, from killing to cooking. The one who taught me used to carry a skewer in his top pocket, and he would inspect the tins when they had been cleaned by poking about in the corners. If everything was not spotless, we got boiling water and started again. I hated it then, but I am grateful to him now. You had to fight for existence. There was always someone ready to take your job for ten shillings a week less.

Grandmother knew …
    … that hot vinegar takes away paint stains.
    … that if boiling water is poured on used tea leaves and the mixture is left for an hour in a bottle, the liquid cleans mirrors and glassware, furniture and linoleum.
    … that a few drops of lemon juice dropped into the water that cleans the lettuce makes it crisp, whereas salt makes it flabby.

... that a little mustard rubbed on to hands after peeling onions removes the smell.

... that cleaning damp shoes is aided by adding a few drops of paraffin to the blacking.

My grandmother was very hard-working, little, and fat, like me. She used to salt her bacon and cure her hams outside in a big trough, and there were always hams hanging up ready to eat. She made her own black puddings in Yorkshire pudding tins and, oh, they were good! That's when somebody killed a pig – we would buy half of it.

The late Helen Bradley, painter, born Lees, Oldham, 1900.

A walker stopped by a small garden whose main crop was cress.

'Would you like some?' asked the gardener.

'I'll not say no,' replied the walker.

The gardener cut a small bunch and said, 'That'll be tuppence.'

The walker was shocked but paid. As he walked away, he called back, 'If I were thee, I'd get that fence mended.'

'Why's that?'

'Because if a sheep gets i'theer, it could do hundreds of pounds' worth of damage.'

10

The Russells of Spring

We went in the back of our veg van and left it at the end of Albert Road so that we could brush off the potato dust and make a stately progress to the white front doors.

The late Russell Harty, broadcaster,
talking about family holidays at Blackpool.

I T IS THE FIRST WHIFF OF SEA after the dark winter. Like a salmon that must seek its river, I feel that some inner need drives me, each year, just before Easter, to Blackpool. I find what I expect to find: a coldness that numbs the senses, a vast and virtually uninhabited space of beach and sea, tartiness of façade, and vulgarity awash in cockly smells; a deadness in which there is, nevertheless, a sense of awakening. Blackpool eyeing the world with uncertain anticipation. Without the unborn there could not be the born, saw wise men of the East, and at this point Blackpool is unborn. The yearly birth is sudden and startling and loud and brash and Easter announces its imminent arrival.

I remember many days like this grey, flat day. I remember an Easter of 1969, a bucketing cold day with few about, and the Monster from the Bowels of the Earth did not appear to be at home on the Golden Mile, though I prodded his lair cautiously. Tommy Catlow was at home, though. At eighty, he had taken to his bed in his little terraced house, because soon he was having visitors off to Canada, and he did not wish to give them a cold for the voyage.

He emerged wearing blue-striped pyjamas in mid-afternoon to talk about this Golden Mile which, in season, became a pretension, a candyfloss, a judder of sound, a splutter of pennies, all of it victim of the new sophistication, the victim of planners' plans and papers.

Four hundred yards long, this Golden Mile; its most baffling trick of all.

Tommy had been associated with it for forty-odd years and on this occasion he began his account of it, 'In the days of long ago ...' Bernard Delfont should have been listening to this but he was in London thinking, maybe, about the Mile himself and what he was going to do about it, for he had become boss of Blackpool show business, and him a Londoner, not sand-bred. They were disappearing, the sand-bred 'uns, even then. Some made a deal of money but they were, for the most part, too big to be small but not big enough to be the biggest. Not big as Delfont with his fingers in Forte and EMI, the piers, the Tower, not like him.

At this stage in Blackpool history – for it is 1969 remember – he is 'thinking' about the Mile, but in any case EMI will be spending £4m or so over four years, which is a lot of rock. Much has gone already, of course: the mock auction men flogging stuff they call 'swag'; the starving people gone from their exhibition cabinets. Ah, the fasters! Brides and grooms plucked from their nuptials and caged away to be peered at for threepence a time: where are they?

Some fasted away quite painfully by day, but ate well by night. Ricardo Sacco – there was a great faster, a ghost of a man, and when he died six weeks after a sixty-five-day fast, to fast either no more or for ever more, the coroner said, 'That's misadventure.' And he did not know the half of it.

Tommy knew Sacco. Sacco was supposed to go with him to Wales for exhibition, but there was a last-minute hitch, so – 'the man running about with advertising boards went in the cage. He was a good turn, but eventually, we wanted him out and he wouldn't come out. He says, "Sacco has got motor cars and I can do this job." I said, "Aye, but you must understand that Sacco is on different terms."'

'A doctor writes a bulletin, "Cardiac failure setting in." Well, people were coming from miles around. I said, "We'd better get somebody from the infirmary or somewhere to verify that he has to come out," and beggar me, if he didn't find a doctor and some students prepared to take him on. I said to them, "You carry the key to the cabinet in case he snuffs it." He lasted another fortnight. Finally, I got the ambulance and we took him to a home and he was there about a fortnight. Then he started to move about again. That was the last of him as far as I knew.'

Al Capone's car (Capone being an American gangster, of course); the bullet-filled body of Jesse James; Moby Dick; Epstein's statues; Kap Dwa, the two-headed giant from Paraguay ... And Zulus ('They'd run in the street, you know. They'd run any dam'd where'). Giraffe-necked women; Blondin, the Niagara Falls tightrope walker; a man who said he was a doctor struck off who could cure anything except his own fat head: all were in or around the Mile.

'Medicine,' said this doctor, 'will not do you any good. You want to go to the water's edge and drink God's clean, fresh air. Still, if it's medicine you want, I can write you a prescription. Sixpence, sir, only sixpence.'

Between two wooden breakwaters, buskers, acrobats, concertina players, ventriloquists, fortune tellers, patent medicine pedlars, Punch and Judy, pie and rock stalls, and donkeys. All operated in tumbling and tangled profusion by the water's edge and they had to retreat when the tide came in. Monsters, minstrels, mind readers, the mad, the magnificent, winkles and whelks and oysters, tacklers with trousers upturned, white, thin legs like lollipop sticks, the little sands of time ...

All this, all these, are minuscule against the central point of the Mile's history, the arrival of the Rev. Harold S. Davidson, Rector of Stiffkey, a defrocked cleric exhibited by one Luke Gannon. Gannon, the most flamboyant showman of all.

The rector was notorious in the early 1930s. He was sacked as a minister for failing to convince his superiors in the Church that his regular visits to London's East End were altogether spiritual. So he returned to his original profession, the stage, with the intention, so he said, of raising funds to appeal against his sacking.

His first appearance on the Golden Mile came in 1932 when he was enlisted for fourteen days to fast inside a barrel. It is said, and believe it if you like for your fivepence, sir, that the reverend gentle-man, not sure whether he liked the idea, stepped inside the barrel merely to try it for size, whereupon Gannon locked the little door and quickly had ten thousand customers at twopence a time. Next day, Gannon and the rector were prosecuted for obstruction and fined £2, but the publicity was worth a fortune.

A group of miners did not think much of the rector and decided to throw him and his barrel into the sea, but they dropped both on the promenade. The corporation would have liked to do something similar, one suspects, because their intention was to make the Golden Mile a more bazaar but less bizarre place. With this in mind, they drafted an Act which gave them the right to close undesirable or offensive exhibitions. Waxworks were excluded so as not to offend Tussaud's and its Chamber of Horrors. Gannon brought the rector back to the Mile shortly before the Act was due to take effect in August 1935, and there the cleric lay in a glass-topped cabinet.

A notice said, 'The ex-Stiffkey rector claims that he will make it his life's end and will fast unto death if his appeal is unheeded.

Police went to close the show and Gannon pointed out that they did not have the power, since he had flanked the entrance by two large wax effigies, one of a mammy-style minstrel and the other of Jack the Ripper. The police retired. The corporation was flummoxed. But its officers came up with a sort of solution: the rector was charged with fasting with intent to kill himself. He was acquitted after a doctor declared him fitter after fasting than he had been before.

The rector exhibited himself in a refrigerated chamber, and in a hothouse. On his final grand appearance, so they say, he lay prostrate in a pit with an automatic clockwork demon tormenting him with a gilded trident. Not, apparently, tormented enough, he finally stepped on the tail of a lion named Freddie in a cage at Skegness and departed this life in 1937, considerably mauled, reputedly having made, and spent, £10,000: a tidy sum for the time.

One of the sand-bred 'uns recalled Gannon showing a man with two heads. 'There wasn't much money about in those days and this visitor is supposed to have said, "Could you make a reduction for quantity?"'

Gannon said, 'How many are there?'

'There's me, the wife and sixteen kids.'

'Stop there,' said Gannon. 'I'll bring the fellow with two heads to see you.'

Mother Kelly's Doorstep, An Egg, an 'Am and an Onion: the song-pluggers were at work ... Jack Hylton, Lawrence Wright, Bert Feldman ...

Tommy Catlow's mind is not on music; it is still concerned with the fasters.

'Speaking of Wales, I had a doctor who used to keep a record of the fasting man, temperature and so on, and what he had drunk, saying whether he was a bit better or a bit worse: daily bulletins.

I remember he came a bit late one day and I said, "Don't waste much time, doctor; we've got a few clients about." So he lifted the shutter, got hold of my wrist by mistake, and said, "Oh, he'll live for ever, he will." '

Here is the showman's paper, *The World's Fair*, and it is all alive yet.

> Wanted in Blackpool for long season and long working hours: ugly man or woman, fat man or woman, tattooed man or woman, midgets, or wax figures for walk-around show.
> Who's for a haunted house on wheels at £400 o.n.o.?

On, to 1973. Again, it is April. South Pier has endured the poundings of the ocean during another winter and now it is deserted apart from Carol Petulengro, Romany clairvoyant, part of the large family of Petulengros. She is prettying up her kiosk during her first visit there since the end of the illuminations.

We meet like explorers in this jungle of wood and silence, she wielding her paintbrush with its matt black paint, and saying (looking deep into my psyche out of habit) that the next eighteen months will provide me with a fortune, which is comforting but, in the retrospection of the 1990s, untrue. She has her regulars and they come back every year and one wonders: Why? Because, she says, she tells them the truth. If there is bad news and she thinks they can take it, she tells them. Accidents she tells them about. Illnesses. But if anyone is going to die she does not suppose they would be told. It takes five minutes to see the essential elements of a person. Her mother was telling fortunes on the front. Her cousin, Eva, was famous in Brighton. And you know what? A Romany can not read another Romany's future.

There are people, ordinary visitors, who go in summer time and she can not read them because they are psychic themselves. She can not tell them anything at all. There is a barrier, and she does not know why.

Beyond her kiosk are virgin acres of sand without footprint, yet millions have walked here, feeling the harsh grains between their toes. Like life, that sand. People here have lisped their first words, heard their own children lisp their words in time, and have taken to the covered shelters of the prom in old age before vanishing for ever, a human tide going out, a human tide ready to wash in, the simple progression of seasons and generations.

Blackpool got its piers because Victorians, with their assumptions of virtue and godliness, liked to have the illusion of walking upon water. More than half of Stanley Park was bought for 4d. a yard, freehold, by Sir Lindsay Parkinson, who thereupon sold it to the corporation at the same price. So the people built it and nurtured it – the sand-grown 'uns, mainly.

Who, now, would have the courage to build a Tower? Once, sixty thousand people a day, on average, passed through its turnstiles, half a crown a time, a shilling for children; and one day in 1949, seventy-five thousand went through.

Bill McGinty, man and boy, remembered the great days. He was a call boy at the Grand Theatre (threatened by demolition, reprieved, gloriously restored), and he became its manager. He became manager of the Tower complex, and moved on to be general manager of Louis Tussaud's waxworks. I leave the beaches to seek him out and he says, 'Once they had a show with a live horse involving a revolving mat which went beneath its feet. The scenery was made to move in the opposite direction and there was an impression of speed, although the horse, theoretically, remained where it was, running. And one night it ended up in the orchestra.'

They had just tested a tape for the Chamber of Horrors and the squeaks, creakings and other elements of weirdness floated across the unseeing exhibits. Long ago, a policeman went for a late-night cup of tea at this waxworks and he was left, temporarily, by a large sink used at the time for the cleaning of exhibits. While he was there, alone, the sink emptied, and such were the suckings and gurglings of the plughole that he fled into the night without saying goodbye.

At a guest house named Roker on the front, an old man has arrived to see his sick friend, and the man who answers the door says, 'Oh, he died, you know,' and the old chap turns around and walks away. 'Why Roker?' I say to the man at the door. And he supposes it is because of Roker Park, where Sunderland play football. Here, another endearing facet of Blackpool: the way landladies create little echoes of their home towns in what they assumed would be their heaven.

Along the front is a lamp post I remember, where two old people were blown round and round in a gale like figures in a Swiss clock. They would have been going yet if the wind had not dropped. A friend noted, in this area, that a child who attacked a Rolls with his spade was told by his mother, 'Don't do that. I'm fed up of buying you spades.' He noted, too, an old couple looking at a joke shop window, and after long study and much thought, the husband nudged his wife and said, 'Hey, let's 'ev one o'them little bundles o'muck.'

I call on a resident watch-maker friend. His name is Jack Ward, since retired. In forty years I have seen him everywhere in Blackpool but on a beach. He is in a back room of the shop, magnifying glass clamped to his eye, as always, and he knows when summer is coming because sand begins to appear in the watches.

Soon the rock men will appear, flinging wide their arms in dismay at the grim procession of plastic macs, for the moment, on the front; there is a not-so-slim lady saying to a friend, 'Let's have a cup of tea, love. We might as well be wet inside as out.' Around the foot balm counter of a store, a group of sufferers listens dully to a salesman who knows his spiel as a bishop does his Twenty-third Psalm.

'I'll have one,' says a middle-aged man in a sudden burst of positive thinking.

'You'll never regret it,' says the spiel.

'Watch out for me,' says his customer. 'Next time I come past here, I'll be running.'

On, now to 1979, and an historic event: Charlie Cairoli, clown, announces his retirement. After thirty-nine years as target for custard pies and buckets of water at Blackpool Tower Circus, his doctor has advised him to 'take it easy'. He is seventy in February and he passes into legend with his red putty nose, his bowler, his fractured English, his immense pride and his remorseless search for perfection: Britain's best-known clown, though the technical term that describes what he does is *auguste*.

No *auguste* will ever again serve such a hard apprenticeship, or have so much demanded of him on stage or off. These days, no-one is required to play several instruments by the time he is five years old; or sleep in a cupboard drawer. Charlie's circus background was regal. Marriage linked him to the legendary Fretallinis. The original Cairolis had their own crest and fought the Saracens. Although he was born in Italy, his parents were born in France. In the modest house he occupied, pictures and plaques bore witness to the vast mosaic of his life: here, Charlie and the queen; there, Charlie and Prince Andrew; over here, a plaque from Monaco; in the basement, medals for this and that. He played to Hitler in Nuremburg. 'He laughed like everybody else, gave me a cigarette case. When war was declared, I threw it into the sea.'

His mother did trapeze, horse riding and – with his father – juggling. His father was clown, musician, and juggler with both hands and feet. They lived in Montmartre, Paris. 'It was a very hard life. When we travelled, my mother would choose a room where there was a big wardrobe so that she could put a pillow in a drawer for my bed. My father said, one day, at a matinee in a little theatre, "Today, you work." And when I finished he said, "Were you scared?" "Scared of what?" "The audience, the lights." And I said, "No." He turned to my mother and said, "We'll never do anything with that one. He has no feeling." '

'But I was blessed. I could always make contact with children more or less straight away. My son's got it. Not everybody can do that.'

As a boy, Cairoli was blacked up and dressed as a page. Then they made him up as an old man. Charlie decided to use his own assets: an astute move because it became impossible to imitate him. He was around top of the bill since the age of seventeen and never once flopped. He clutched a handful of letters. 'Look at these,' he said, 'they're all addressed to Charlie Cairoli, Angleterre.' A year later, in 1980, he died, aged seventy.

On, on to the high summer of 1984 ...

When August fills the asphalt with an endless sea of feet, Blackpool Pleasure Beach, Europe's greatest amusement park, gets down to the absorbing business of separating a man from his money. It manages to make the act both painless and pleasurable. In this year of 1984, Doris Thomson is eighty-one and high summer is a prospect she has never ceased to view with joy. Her life encompasses the three men who created all this: her father, W. G. Bean, whose principle was 'to make adults feel like children'; her dignified husband, Leonard Thomson who, when a number of bikini-clad girls were pointed out to him, said, 'But where do they keep their money?'; and her son, Geoffrey Thomson, who became managing director. A family affair.

Doris had remained chairman, remembering a strict father who wore goggles to keep blowing sands from his eyes, and a husband she accompanied to far places in search of entertainment ideas.

She was born in Great Yarmouth but went to Blackpool at the age of six weeks. Her father was born in London, went to America at nineteen, stayed a few years and worked as an amusement park engineer, then came back with the Hotchkiss Bicycle Railway, a mechanical ride. He was bursting with ideas. Here was a strict man, well-read, a good speaker, affectionate, and he teamed up with a friend, John W. Outhwaite, a meat trader from Shipley, in Yorkshire, to develop amusements at South Shore. To do this, they bought forty acres of sands. Outhwaite died in 1911 and his interests passed to his two sons, but Bean had always been the dominant partner.

The Big Dipper came in the 'twenties: a gravity coaster with five almost-sheer drops of fifty feet and with a wooden structure more than three thousand feet long built from American pitch pine. Bean charged a shilling a ride, which seemed an enormous sum. 'But my father said, "For that I am giving them a mahogany pay desk and a terrazzo entrance."'

He used to say, 'Never despise your bread and butter. It is all right having highfalutin' ideas, but when you come right down to it, you have to know where your next meal is coming from.'

Her dignity, then, and later, was that of an elite. When she tried the rides (two trips on the Dipper without a break at eighty-one) it was not affectation. She had done it all her life. 'I had to be involved. I had to be a rider.'

When Doris married, her husband 'who had seen me waiting on father thought I would do the same for him, and I said, "Ah, that's different. I'm not doing it for a husband."'

The Dipper, then, was her father's, the National her husband's. From the start, it all just grew and grew: River Caves of the World, Velvet Coaster, Joy Wheel, a Naval Spectatorium (1910) using a combination of 360-degree projection and mechanical devices to recreate the Battle of Monitor and Merrimac, the first encounter between the ironclads in the American Civil War.

'I used to go regularly to hear a very important-looking gentleman in a top hat who gave the commentary. He used to call it the first battle of the eye-ron clads. The pronunciation always amused me. They finished that show with the naval review off Spithead, which looked very fine. But if you went behind the scenes, those ships sailing along in such a dignified manner amid rolling waves were on wheels and were being pushed by a man who also fired the guns.'

There used to be a little stage on a roll-top desk, all lit up, and with tiny people dancing. 'Of course, they were fully grown, but with this mirror idea, I believed they were real. I was always begging to play with them. My father said they were temperamental people and would be upset.'

She supposed that people of this age were less childlike and that sophistication came earlier in life. But some things remained constant. The Dipper, altered, but basically the same; the National still popular; the River Caves still valid; the flying machines keeping their appeal. So Blackpool had run its course from fasters and fatties and midgets and horrors to buttons and levers and fitted carpets and Doris Thomson remembered all that was worth remembering. She looked out on this vast investment rolling away into the far distance, huge, gaudy, loud, magnificent, the flagship for their other amusement parks in Morecambe, Southport and America and laughed at the thought of the Scottish family, one of whose members looked at that very scene and asked, 'Will the fair be here next week, too?'

My father was manager on the West End pier at Morecambe for a time. Then he moved to the Alhambra, which was a step up. After that, he moved two steps up and went to the Royalty Theatre and a house was included in his wage. I could play on the stage in the mornings whenever I wanted to. I worked with my dad and when I was nearly fifteen a Mr Blundell knocked at our front door and said to my mother, 'They need an assistant at our shop and she seems a very smart young lady.' Blundell's were drapers – shrouds, ties, modesty vests, you name it. I went the first morning and cleaned the yard measure, which was made of brass. Hat pins from before the Victorian period were there. Glorious. I used to have to do them with emery paper. I cleaned the shop floor front to back: thirty-two boxes at the back with brass handles and no metal polish to touch the boxes. Dark knickers to be worn because there were ladders to be climbed. Navy blue dresses. Black silk stockings. Mrs Blundell was a character out of a Dickensian play, like a tram ticket sideways, she was that thin, and she terrified me.

Thora Hird, actress.

A tackler on his motor-bike stopped at traffic lights. Said a passing pedestrian, 'Do you know your back light is missing?'

'Beggar t'light,' said the tackler. 'Where's t'wife and sidecar?'

Variation: Tackler riding at seventy miles an hour through Preston is hailed by a pedestrian: 'Hey, your lass has fallen off t'back of t'bike.'

Tackler: 'Never mind, I'll get another in Blackpool.'

A group of Lancastrians at New York's airport, still in their caps. 'Are you looking for your Mary? Who's just gone up in t'hoist.'

(True.)

A couple heading for America by ship boarded the Liverpool ferry by mistake and arrived in Birkenhead dragging their luggage.

'Where are you from?' asked a passer-by and the reply came, 'We're from England, t'best little country in t'world.'

Boy and girl walked from sea to beach at Blackpool and realised they knew each other.

'It's not Mary, is it?'

'It is.'

'Mary from Smith Street?'

'The same.'

'You know me – Joe. I live in t'next street to you. Where are you staying?'

'Mrs Brown's.'

'I'm staying at Mrs Brown's. Which room are you in?'

'Number seven.'

'I'm in number six. Hey, how about a few drinks tonight, just you and me, then back to my room for a coffee …'

'Well, maybe, but let's get back in t'watter. Everybody can see what we're talking about.'

Blackpool, a works trip, and a number of tacklers out for a paddle.

'By gum, Jack,' says one, 'tha has nasty [dirty] feet.'

'Aye,' says Jack, 'but I didn't come on t'trip last year.'

David Lee, Haslingden.

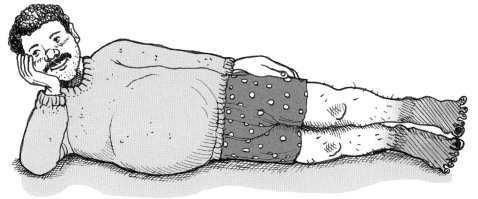

First variation, Frank Randle: 'So I went to see this chiropody fellow and he says, "Take your socks off," and I said, "They are off," and he said, "By heck, thi feet are nasty," and I said, "I bet thine are nasty," and he said, "Yes, but I'm not as old as thee." '

Second variation: Two tacklers bathing at Blackpool.
   'I'll tell you what Jack, you didn't half want a wash.'
   'Did I? Don't forget, I'm three years older than thee.'

Two tacklers decided to holiday in the countryside rather than go to Blackpool. They then found that they had forgotten to pack pillows. They looked around for substitutes and found two drainpipes. Next morning, one had a stiff neck. He complained to his companion and said, 'How did you get on?'
   'Grand, you see, I stuffed mine wi' straw.'

Two tacklers watched an aircraft in flight for the very first time.
   'By heck,' said one, 'that's amazing.'
   'It is, too,' said his friend, 'but what bothers me is how they'll climb out up theer if owt goes wrong wi' t'engine.'

A tackler on tour by motor-bike receiving his bill for bed and breakfast at an inn:
   'That's fine, but what about the bike?'
   'I usually charge a shilling for a horse,' said the landlord.
   'Well,' said the tackler, 'my bike it two-and-a-half horsepower, so here's half a crown.'

Tackler Joe and his wife, Sarah, loved to go to Blackpool for their holidays but did not like admitting where they had been to neighbours, who preferred to go abroad. Returning from Blackpool, Sarah said, 'You know, Joe, they will all be bragging about where they've been on Monday morning and all we can talk about is t'Tower. Why don't we say we've been abroad?'
   'Champion,' said Joe.
   Sure enough, he was asked the question on Monday morning. 'Italy,' he replied. 'That's where we went, didn't we love?'
   'Oh, it was marvellous,' said Sarah. 'We went by coach. There were these great mountains and passes, so high you felt you were flying. Then all those vines and fine buildings. Something we'll never forget. And Rome. The Vatican. It was fantastic, that was. Pope came out

himself, all dressed in white, and we happened to have got on t'front row and he had a special word with me and Joe and we got on so well. Later on, he saw us in t'pub and he recognised us and came over and we chatted for a long time. He bought Joe a pint and me a Snowball. Lovely fellow. Can't help but like him. But *her* ...!'

A tackler on holiday in London noticed, on booking into an hotel, that some names had initial letters behind them.

'Why is that?' he asked the receptionist.

'Those are honours, sir.'

So he wrote his name and added T.B.B.T.I.B.

'What's that stand for?' asked the receptionist and he replied, 'T'best bloody tackler i' Blackburn.'

A party of people heading for their parked coach late at night after a day out in Blackpool came across a friend much the worse for drink and helped him along the prom and into the vehicle. An hour later, they had him propped against the door of his home and were trying to awaken whoever might be inside. A window shot up.

'Who's that?'

'We've brought Jack home. He'd had a drink or two ...'

'Where from?'

'Blackpool.'

'You shouldn't have done. He'd gone for a fortnight.'

A coach party looking for their vehicle late at night after a few drinks at Blackpool found themselves on the front, lost. There was a solitary light in the blackness of the far distance. One member said, 'That's t'direction, I'm sure.' So they headed for the light and after an hour's steady walking realised they were no nearer and that it was a boat heading for Fleetwood.

(True.)

A Lancastrian taken on hurriedly as a waiter aboard a luxury cruise ship found himself inconvenienced by a large dinner table in the first class restaurant.

'Hands up,' he said, 'them as wants coffee.'

He was fired.

11

TREADLING A GOAT

T HE LANCASHIRE OF WEFT, WARP AND WEAVERS was also a place where, if fun were not invented, it scarcely existed at all. Fun did not come down a wire or out of the sky and it was no worse for that: it lay in such things as running and jumping, wrestling and reading; in going to conversaziones (concerts: and whatever happened to *them*?), in feats of various kinds – of eating prodigiously or fasting relentlessly – or wrestling bears at fairs (a Lancastrian who wrestled one such animal is alleged to have said, on being defeated, 'I'd have beaten yon mon if he'd taken his fur coat off').

Newspapers reflected this fun, and they thrived on old customs. Journalists and public doted on them. As a trainee journalist on what was then called *The Northern Daily Telegraph*, I had a news editor named T. C. Colling, who employed me at £1 a week, but only after asking how many languages I spoke. I could speak two at the time: English and dialect, neither particularly well, but I said three, and included French, because my guess was that he would be either unable or unwilling to put me to the test. I was right.

I watched him mellowing and whitening down the years, and somewhere in this time he became an old customs man. He knew, as I knew, that people love old customs like they love their dogs. They harbour them in far-off recesses of the mind to be stroked in silent recollection, or in pub talk. Somewhere in old tin boxes, a man will keep yellowing cuttings of some claim, monstrous or otherwise.

T. C.'s name was Cuthbert, but he was never anything other than Mr Colling to everyone, including his second wife. In due time, he became a victim of mine. I had moved to what journalists call 'the nationals' and he still sat at his desk concerned with East Lancashire both past and present.

Old customs are minefields for the unwary. Consider treadling a goat, grain humping, huffling a pig, or going to watch a dancing troupe known as the Britannia Cocoanutters. It takes a clever, possibly a three-language, man to discern the true and false in them.

Treadling a goat is an invention of mine. There is no such thing. So is grain humping at Preston Docks. Huffling a pig ... well, I am not sure myself about that. If you believe that Lancastrians in pubs kicked a pig around in stockinged feet then you believe in huffling. The Britannia Cocoanutters existed and, so far as I know, exist yet. They find pleasure in dancing around with blackened faces.

I had been bemused for some time by newspaper pictures of old men with big moustaches standing at the doors of butchers' shops. The captions were similar: 'Little would you guess that this is now where the new town hall stands,' and so on. I wrote to T. C. a letter which proceeded something like this:

> It has no doubt come to your notice that in the old days, there was a custom on Haslingden moors known as bunting, or treadling, a goat. You will remember it well. The idea was that you put a number of iron hoops in the ground and the first man to bunt, or treadle, a goat through all the hoops without the goat's horns touching the tops or sides was awarded a hot barm cake and a pint of mulled ale.
>
> I well recall an old gentleman named John o'Jacks who was a champion bunter. One day he turned up for a match a bit the worse for drink, so that instead of bunting the goat, the goat bunted him.
>
> Laugh! We did laugh, sir! It so happens that I still have my old treadling irons and I thought you might like to look at them, but I would be much obliged if you could return them, as they are of great sentimental value.

The treadling irons were, in fact, hoops from brewery barrels, large, ungainly things kindly provided by the then landlord, Bill Martland, of the Adelphi pub across the road from the newspaper office. I delivered them to the front counter and left them there. The letter bore a fictitious name and a non-existent address on Haslingden moor, which is vast and possibly uncharted. I then had the satisfaction of seeing my old custom printed in full and in black type and waited for years for it to appear in an authentic book on old Lancashire. It never did, and I was surprised.

As for the hoops, I have no doubt that T. C. returned them and I had a vision of an old postman somewhere in the moorland grass, trudging about at the age of 103 wondering what in God's name he was carrying on his back and trying to find an address totally unknown to the GPO. At this late stage, I apologise to him for involving him in something which was none of his business.

Being the inventor of an old custom gives one panache. I was encouraged by the experience and decided to take on another old customs expert employed by the same newspaper. Whenever Harry Kay was short of material for his weekly column, he would trot out a lengthy story about a man named Jack Higgins, a jumper, and pretend that someone had written in inquiring about him.

Jack Higgins was a remarkable jumper, and he certainly existed. He could leap across a canal, put out a lighted candle floating in the middle with one foot, and land on the other bank without apparent effort. He could also jump over heaven-knows-how-many barrels, and there were pictures to prove it. One of these pictures was printed so many times that the metal block was almost worn away. The story always ended with the same words (since the story was never re-written): 'He was a jumper was Jack Higgins.'

I wrote a letter to Harry Kay, a former sports editor and man of great humour, and it went something like this:

> Whatever happened to the humpers at Preston Docks? Many's the time I remember, as a child, seeing them carrying their huge sacks of grain from the cargo boats in endless procession, moaning their old Lancashire songs ... 'Hook and carry, hook and carry.' My old grandfather was one of the first humpers and the only man who could carry two sacks at one go. Hack was his name. Hack Jiggins. He was known far and near for his exploits among the humpers, and even at the age of ninety-four he was still to be seen humping his two sacks and moaning those old songs.
>
> Well, one day, he was humping and he went between the ship and dockside in an almighty splash, and some said it was the drink, and some said it was his age, but he never really got back into form again and he has gone into legend with others of his kind.

The last sentence read, 'He was a humper, was Hack Jiggins.'

I was surprised when the whole letter was printed and not a word was said. Not one contradiction. I met Harry Kay in the pub some time later and he just stared at me, laughing gently. I suppose he guessed the truth of the matter, but he made no reference to it.

I never paid much attention to old customs in my early days, possibly because my time was taken up with visiting ancient people who mumbled in front of their fires and remembered strange and uninteresting things. One, asked by a colleague what had been his most memorable experience in a long life, said, 'Shifting all t'looms from one mill to another during one weekend.'

'Fancy,' said my friend, 'living all that time and his best memory is of behaving like a donkey.'

T. C. was always an indecipherable writer. I was given one of his cryptic instructions and deciphered it to my own satisfaction, which is how I came to have the following conversation:

'Is Eric o'Marble Head in, please?'

'Eric o'who?'

'Marble Head.'

'If you mean Eric o'Marmalade, that's me dad and he's sitting by t'fire. Come inside and have some currant cake.'

I do not recall the rest of the conversation but they were all much the same.

'This lad's from t'papers, dad.'

'Eh?'

'Papers.'

'How much is it?'

'No, he's come from t'paper now that you're a hundred.'

'Ah!'

'What does it feel like to be a hundred?'

'Bloody cold.'

'Yes.'

'T'king sent a telegram.'

He would.

It occurred to T. C. eventually that I was just the man to be a drama critic, on what grounds I will never know. I quickly established ground-rules for this post. First, since I knew nothing of drama – theatres not being thick on the ground in Oswaldtwistle – I would, on each occasion when asked to perform my duties, look up the play in a reference book. Second, since all the actors and actresses were readers of the newspaper, the authors were to be criticised, not them. Third, to lend dignity and authority to my literary pieces, I would include a couple of lines of verse, preferably by an obscure, but eminent, poet whom everyone had heard of, but whom few had read except in snippets. Cuthbert Colling knew nothing of my ground rules, but he obviously approved the result. On the whole, that is. A typical piece might begin:

> How this play, performed last night by Accrington Arts Club, ran for 1,237 performances in New York, I shall never know.

Next came a couple of lines from Byron or Coleridge or, if I felt particularly majestic, Milton, followed by:

> Jane Smith was superb in the leading role and it is a pity that her delicate artistry was not better supported by the author, whose lack of cohesion and purpose was particularly noticeable in the second act.

Thus I achieved something of a reputation without the need for any literary knowledge whatsoever. On the strength of it, I bought a trilby and a long mackintosh and adopted a raffish air on trams in the manner of a Hannen Swaffer. I would have grown a moustache had my upper lip been equal to the task.

Cuthbert Colling was visibly impressed. He had never heard of the poems I quoted (neither, for that matter, had I); nor did he assume that I never knew, immediately, and without reference to anyone, the precise performance record of each play in any major capital. But in the back of his mind he must have suspected that I was a bit over the top, because he would appear at the reporters' room door and go through a ritualistic dialogue:

'Blackburn Arts Club tonight, Mr Mather: 250 words.'

'Yes, Mr Colling.'

'Tickets in my office when you are ready.'

'Yes, Mr Colling.'

He would then turn on his heel and exit. The door would open again. His face would reappear.

'Oh, and Mr Mather.'

'Yes, Mr Colling.'

'No poetry.'

I was in awe of him, as most people were. Such minor disasters as I have described are taken out of context and therefore distort the normal picture of competence and integrity.

He married his secretary, a splendidly perceptive and admirable woman named Cissie Fine, late in life. She was known to all as Miss Fine. The marriage was kept secret until they had returned from honeymoon, and at that stage someone in the office said, 'How's it going, Mr Colling?'

'All right,' he said. 'Nice to be back at work. I've left Miss Fine at home.'

In turn, they died, and Blackburn Boulevard, where the old newspaper office stood, took on new shapes and things and nothing is as it was. A supermarket has sprouted and it has a café. I reckoned I had a coffee in what was the old machine room, which I first saw at the age of seventeen when the chief reporter had a nose bleed and called for a spanner to cool his blood and stem the flow. I was given one three feet long. 'Take it back, take it back,' he was crying as I tried to get it down the back of his collar.

Old ghosts stir where once that building stood and they will be tangible in my memory until I, too, am a memory.

It was an old custom to put the corpse in the front room and have the neighbours around for a bit of a stare. ('He's left that sideboard to our Nellie, and she never lifted a finger when he suffered.')

It was an old custom to get new sheets, pillowcases, cardigans, scarves, gloves and pack them neatly into bottom drawers where they would never again see daylight: too good to be used, they lay in waiting for the heirs.

It was an old custom to polish the tramlines outside your own home and sandstone all the steps and window ledges.

It was an old custom in pubs to turn your glass upside down when your friend was slow to pay, saying, 'I've supped up – have I done wrong?'

It was an old custom to strike first and then ask questions.

So old customs are good or bad according to the individual recollection. All in all, I would rather invent them, and with the passing of the old customs men, that is denied me now.

I once had a phone call from an outlying district reporting the death of a vicar. There was just time to write the report and catch the first edition, which was produced around midday. As the presses rolled, I stood with T. C. Colling in his boulevard-front office and the two of us watched the vicar ride by. He looked quite pert in his cycle clips. 'What shall we do, Mr Colling?' I asked.

He thought awhile, then said, 'Put him in t'births, next edition.'

Selection of newspaper advertisements appearing in East Lancashire when the cotton industry was thriving and tacklers were everywhere:

You can't be optimistic with a misty optic.

(Optician.)

You may escape me now, but I'll nail you in the end.

(Funeral undertaker.)

Why walk about half dead when you can be buried for ten quid?

(Same undertaker.)

No-one is bakin'
such good bread as Makin.

Local newspaper headline: 'LESS DRUNKENNESS AT CHURCH' [a place near Accrington]'. *Punch* magazine, quoting it: 'Keep it up, keep it up.'

The bride, for stealing a hen, was dressed in blue organza ...

Local newspaper.

The Queen Mother, after launching the ship, floated stern-first up the river.

Local newspaper.

Firemen were tackling the blaze when a pig bit through the hose.

The fire burned a hole in the floor. In the room below, there was a hole in the ceiling.

Caption beneath a picture of a large ship: 'A tern eagle on her nest.'

Caption elsewhere, beneath a picture of a large and tetchy-looking bird: 'Ship unloading grain at Liverpool Docks.'

The police constable was proceeding through the town centre late at night when he noticed three youths approaching. One tapped the officer's chest. The officer said, 'Desist tapping,' whereupon the youth pushed him over a garden wall and he disappeared. A woman who had observed the incident approached the youth and said, 'Don't you think this has gone far enough?'

Account, c. 1940, sent to an evening newspaper
describing a Saturday night fracas.

In the days when all goalkeepers were described as 'custodians' a Nelson reporter had a lurid turn of phrase – so lurid that his colleagues frequently had difficulty in deciding what he meant. They translated 'the rosy rubicund fruit' (correctly) as a tomato, but were stumped when they came to 'this votary of the hammer, chisel and gluepot.' It turned out to be a joiner.

'Thirties local journalist, a man of great knowledge, on being asked whether he would attend a lecture in town by the world's greatest authority on Shakespeare: 'No.'
  'Why?'
  'Shakespeare is dead.'

The same man, being told that a cat was stranded on a high railway parapet, with the fire brigade in attendance, all town centre traffic stopped, and a man risking his life on a narrow ledge armed with a long brush to retrieve the animal: 'I'm not bothering with it.'
  'Why not?'
  'I've got six cats at home and nobody gives a damn about them.'

A journalist was in the habit of playing cards with friends while the weekend edition was being prepared. If he was losing, he would scoop up the cards, walk to the street, and post them down the nearest drain. When he played a game of golf with his editor and was losing, he broke his club across one knee, and marched off the course crying, 'If you want the town council covering, cover it your bloody self.'

'I am going to Bordeaux for my holidays,' said a reporter.
  'Who's Dough?' asked his friend.

'Drunk again, Pilkington,' cried an editor to a reporter, peering through the hatchway between best bar and vault during working hours, and Pilkington, a man noted for his convivial habits, cried back, 'Aye, so am I, Fred.'

A journalist I once described as opening the drinking for England against Australia at Old Trafford (he beat a Sydney judge and a retired Australian Test player by two large gins and a tonic after taking the new glass at ten) felt the need, one hot summer lunchtime, to join people lying on the grass in a park. He was the better, and the worse, for a high intake of alcohol. When he awoke, it was dark. Everyone had gone. He was aware of a face close to his. 'Are you all right, sir?' asked the face, which belonged to a park keeper.

'Perfectly all right,' said the journalist. 'I just nodded off.'

He got up and walked away and was surprised to find himself in an ornamental lake. Not wishing to demean himself by retracing his steps past the park keeper, he continued and emerged at the other side of the lake waterlogged. When he arrived home, his wife said, 'Why are you drenched?'

'Because,' he said, 'there was a sudden, sharp shower.'

'What,' she said, 'from the knees down?'

An editor's wife who received a phone call saying that he would be staying longer in Dublin than he anticipated immediately called a cab and went to Manchester Airport. She suspected, probably correctly, that his reason for staying was Dublin's amiable propensity for stout. When the aircraft her husband should have boarded arrived, she waited for the captain and beat him over the head with her umbrella. 'It's all your fault,' she said, 'you shouldn't have left him there.'

12

CAPTAIN COURAGEOUS

'A VERY CURIOUS and, on the whole, a very droll scene occurred at Haslingden on Saturday night last,' reported the *Bolton Chronicle* of 3 February 1827. 'The good and loyal people of that town and neighbourhood to the amount, as it is estimated, of about 300, had assembled at the church as a testimony of their respect to the memory of the late Duke of York.

'The church was not, as we are informed, very brilliantly lighted up – 35 candles just illuminated the interior of the edifice, which gave it a truly sepulchral appearance. Doubtless this was the effect intended, not, as we dare to imagine, from any notice of parochial economy, but to be in accordance with the solemnity of the occasion.

'The Rev. William Gray, the minister, had proceeded in the service as far as the Psalms, and arrived at a particular verse which some irreverent jesters considered to be appropriate to the occasion, when down fell, not the gallery, nor the organ, nor the pulpit, but a small piece of plaster from under the gallery into a pew where some females were sitting.

'An electric spark could not have produced a more instantaneous operation. Imagination pictured the whole edifice as tumbling about their ears. They screamed and did all the etceteras which women in a state of alarm will do. Locks, bolts and bars under such circumstances became mere straws. The pew doors were burst open: a general rush for safety was the immediate consequence, and as the window was the most convenient aperture for some, they sallied through it, but the man who first made the breach cut his hand in the attempt.

'A detachment of the 36th Foot was in the gallery, and Captain Cairns, who was sitting at that side of it opposite to his men, hearing this extraordinary confusion, made nothing of pews, forms, or seats, but gallantly cleared all, placed himself by the side of his men and valiantly drew his sword and ordered them to fix bayonets.

'The carabineers also drew their swords and the church presented the appearance of being in a state of defence against a mighty vendetta attack. The confusion still kept increasing. Those in the gallery rushed to the stairs, down which they went as swift as "shot out of a gun barrel", tumbling over one another in the most grotesque and ludicrous manner imaginable. A rather stout gentleman in the body of the church lustily, and in the agony of his fright, cried out, "Oh, my chilther, my chilther. Let me come out. I have got two little chilther at home." He had a wife, too, but it would appear that in the conglomeration of his ideas, he forgot her. This is rather strange, for we believe that most husbands good, bad, and indifferent, have more reason to remember their wives than any other part of their establishment. But we are forgetting the worthy clergyman. It will be remembered that, on a similar occasion of alarm a short time since, he, with Moses, was the first to fly, but now he was the last. He stuck heroically to his desk, unmoved, and with the most significant signs and gestures, earnestly exhorted the congregation to be quiet, as the church was in danger. He was emblematically supported by Captain Cairns, who had then left the gallery and stood by the side of the reading desk with his sword still drawn until order was restored.

'The inimitable pencil of Hogarth, or the caricaturing power of Cruickshank or Rowlandson, could scarcely have done justice to the scene, the effect of which was heightened by the sombre appearance of the church. There was just light enough to throw a mezzo-tint cast upon the pallor and consternation depicted on almost every countenance. Hats, bonnets and shawls suffered in the general wreck and many an exchange was made, by no means of mutual benefit to both parties. The service was, at length, resumed and the worthy clergyman got safely through his sermon.'

A Rossendale Volunteer could not recollect which was his right leg and which his left. One was wrapped with hay and one with straw, so that instead of the order, 'Left, right, left,' the words, 'Hay leg, straw leg, hay leg' were used.

Major Halstead, a noted raconteur, speaking in 1900.

(Writer Chris Aspin, who tracked down this story, recalls speaking to a former Russian officer whose men had similar problems so that their trouser legs were coloured red and blue.)

And Jesus sat beneath the juniper tree, for he was fair fagged aht.

Local preacher.

Old-time church warden entering an Oswaldtwistle church and refusing a donation to a boy collecting for charity: 'I am a servant of the Lord.'

Notice on door of a much loved and admired doctor, Joseph Douglas Farquhar, Oswaldtwistle, *c.* 1930: 'If you feel half as ill as I do, you will go home to bed.'

Notice in the same doctor's surgery when a younger doctor began to work in the town: 'If anyone wants to go to the miracle doctor, he can bloody well do so.'

13

TROUSERS ANONYMOUS

ALL OVER THE NORTH there are men of advanced years whose trousers come half way up their chests, although they are less frequently seen as years go by. These trousers can not, if the evidence of shop windows is to be believed, be bought. No-one will admit to making them or selling them. And yet there they are, parading the streets, a source of bafflement to all who observe them. At a stroke, they dispense with the need for a jacket. The foulest winters have never breached them. They would have deflected gunfire at Ypres.

As if one mystery were not enough, there is a second. These trousers are suspended from tiny braces, which are also not observed in shops. These are midget braces, minuscule things matching the tiny clogs people exhibit on their sideboards.

The combination of the two intrigues historians, social commentators and tailors, bespoke or otherwise, everywhere.

I asked a tailor whether he had ever been asked for such trousers. He had not. They baffled him as they baffle everyone else. He suggested that, perhaps, the owners left them to members of their families in wills, to be held in perpetuity like stately properties. Perhaps, he added, they were part of a job lot from another century which refused to wear out. Maybe, once upon a time, a gentleman went to be fitted who had eight-foot legs and a one-foot body and the establishment he patronised made up a large batch in error. It was not really for him to say. After thirty years in the trade, bustling about with chalk and tape measure, the mystery was beyond him. But he once had a farmer who carefully chose his fabric for trousers from a pattern book intended for thick overcoats.

The tailor protested that, if he were able to create the trousers, it would be like wearing a quilt. The farmer insisted. The tailor pointed out that no creases would ever adorn these trousers. They would hang like cylinders from the braces, perhaps even restricting leg movement or the circulation of blood when the farmer was involved in milking, goat chasing or such other simple rural pursuits as came his way while encumbered by an excess of fabric. The farmer again persisted, against all the tailor's arguments, and was observed, later, walking stiff-legged around town, happy with the arrangement, his knee joints in a permanently locked position, much like Sir Alec Guinness when he came out of the hot box in *Bridge on the River Kwai*.

This leads me to another sartorial yardstick: the Great Lancashire Bargain.

There is hardly anyone in the county who can resist the massive price reductions frequently offered by enterprising traders, and this sensitivity to a bargain transcends all classes, income groups, and common sense. The insecurities of the 'thirties stalk the land like ghosts.

The Tommy Ball shoe emporium, housed in an old Blackburn factory, is hardly of this ilk: its bargains are genuine and attract coachloads of solid citizens from all over England and Yorkshire. But there is a quirkiness, even here, and it lies in the fact that each pair of shoes is connected by a piece of string which passes through holes made at the back. It has, therefore, become something of a cult thing at parties to try to observe the backs of people's shoes, and the wearers are well aware of that cult.

I have observed the rear of Tommy Ball's own shoes. They did not have holes where the string had been.

Shoes are not, in general, a great problem. Suits are. A professional man found an establishment where the goods on sale were said to be slightly marred by faults, and he noted a remarkable jacket, beautifully cut, and, what is better, fitting him perfectly. He was about to buy the entire suit when the proprietor asked whether he would not, first, like to try on the trousers in a cubicle. The professional man said he saw no reason to; he was obsessed by the quality of the jacket. The proprietor, a man of kindly disposition who knew better, insisted. The professional man emerged from the cubicle in some dismay. One trouser leg was half way up his calf, the other was of standard length; the seat of the trousers protruded like a massive balloon, and stood proud of his own, generous figure of its own volition. From his description, it would appear that he looked like Grock, the clown, as he proceeded. He seemed to be towing something. It reminded him of Les Dawson's proposition that one could never drown in an old-fashioned swimming costume, since the waterlogged wool caused the garment to drag through the surface water yards behind the wearer, like a great cloud of plankton. Reluctantly, he returned the suit to its rack and mused on the kind of deformed human being who would manage to occupy it with dignity in the future.

A terrible malady in Lancashire is the weak chest. Doctors do not diagnose the condition; mothers invariably do so. 'He's always had a weak chest,' they will say of some unfortunate offspring wrapped in brown paper, or worse, from birth. As a child, I had a friend with whom I necessarily shared a room on some family social occasion, and he had what his mother described as a weak chest. He was encased from neck to ankles in thick, greyish material, manufactured to a stiff consistency, and meant to be applied between the skin and whatever else was available for outerwear. I asked him some simple question as he was staring from the window at the morning light, and he turned to answer. The body moved without affecting the stance of the material in the slightest. He revolved within it. The material had an existence of its own, guided by another intelligence. He stared at me and the material continued to view the outside world. Or so I assumed at the time. Such garments are part of an immaculate conception.

A Lancashire journalist went for his army medical examination at the start of the Second World War and failed it, so that he continued his occupation. Some time later, a colleague met one of the army examiners and asked him whether he remembered the man. 'I do,' he said. 'He had the smallest chest and the cleanest feet of anyone I have ever seen in my life.' It is a commendation devoutly to be missed. I imagine that was a weak chest. At any rate, the journalist spent the period of hostilities eating peanut butter to give him strength, and his legs were often encased in leather up to the knees. He would have looked like a dehydrated Storm Trooper, a victim of some atrocity, had the Nazis ever arrived.

An executive was seated in his office when he heard the cry, 'Bargains!' He joined the ragged charge of varying ranks of his colleagues to an establishment nearby where a goodly crowd was already flinging great mounds of trousers and jackets into the air in a frenzied attempt to find a good match. Being an executive, he did not dally about, but clutched trousers and jacket, paid, and headed back to his office, where he hid his purchase in a cupboard so as to retain his dignity and pretend he had not joined the rummage in the first place.

That night, he tried on his suit and it was a perfect fit. All was well, except that one sleeve had obviously come from another jacket of different colour and texture. The sight of himself in the mirror did not please him. He could not lose face by returning the garment. Had he been a more humble person he would, I imagine, have taken the risk, but he had a proper concern for his status. Therefore, he hung the suit in his cupboard and wrote it off as a mistake.

Shortly afterwards, he was sitting in his office, door open, when along the corridor walked a man of intermediate rank, an inferior. This man was in a bargain suit. Everything about it was perfect apart from one sleeve. The sleeve undoubtedly came from the executive's jacket: a match. Furthermore, the odd sleeve on the executive's jacket would have made whole the other man's suit.

What to do? The executive thought awhile, and decided that although an underling might wear a suit with the wrong sleeve, he could not confront him with the fact; even less could he admit to having the underling's correct sleeve in his cupboard at home.

He decided to let his colleague continue to look awry on duty and said nothing to draw attention to himself. It was a wise decision worthy of his rank and status, and no-one was surprised when he was promoted to take charge of an area headquarters.

I have, myself, been the victim of a bargain. Together with a dozen or so national newspaper journalists, I was offered a suit-length of black material for a laughably small sum. I accepted, as did all the others. I was then recommended to a small tailor in the centre of Manchester; small, that is, in business terms. Physically, he was a large and argumentative tailor, much given to waving sharp scissors. At any rate, he viewed the cloth curiously, felt it, then declared that it was not cloth at all. 'I do not know what it is,' he said. 'I only know that it is not cloth.' It looked like cloth to me. It fell in folds and so forth and had an observable texture. I advised him to get on with his measurements and not to be hasty or intemperate during his calculation of the inside leg.

'Where do you usually get your suits?' he asked.

'Hector Powe,' I replied.

'He does a good suit, does Hector,' said the tailor.

He finally produced a garment that fitted and I wore it to work. My friends were similarly attired. We soon found we had a problem. Any crease put into the material stayed there for ever. There was no way of erasing it. No amount of ironing touched it. I concluded that the tailor was probably right. It was not cloth. I was wearing something alien; perhaps a bakelite substance meant for making long-playing records, perhaps some kind of experimental dustbin liner. My friends and I dispensed with our suits immediately and ostracised the photographer who had sold them to us. He, poor fellow, persuaded his wife to have a skirt made from the surplus and the problem became my wife's. She volunteered to make the skirt.

A tackler suffering from rickets and who, as a result, had bowed legs, went to be measured for a suit. The tailor, trying hard not to be offensive, seemed ill at ease measuring the legs.

'Don't bother thisself about that,' said the tackler. 'Just make t'trousers straight. I'll bend 'em.'

14

Not so light, but fantastic

I occasionally watch bands of graceful Lancastrians in formation dancing and wonder from whence they came. It seems incongruous, perhaps even incredible, that they should have been born within the sound of bow legs.

Lancashire and dancing, in my own experience, have little in common, perhaps nothing in common. From a woman's point of view there is sense in that. If you get half a ton of clog-iron against your shin, the experience is rather like meeting a tank head on. There is no point in describing it as the light fantastic.

In the late 1930s it was considered cissy to actually learn. Victor Silvester would have been stoned in our neighbourhood. When boys took to the dance floor, they did so like rugby players caught without trousers at a girl guide convention – blushing and threshing their legs about as if their soles were burning. Had they been caught performing in this manner in any other place and under different circumstances, no doctor in the land would have had difficulty in diagnosing a fit. Only girls learned to dance, and they danced with each other until the last waltz when the floor became packed. At this stage, the lads, bubbling with pints of Thwaites, Dutton's and Lion, leapt into the arena like demons, grabbing what they could before the women vanished into the night. Anywhere else, it would have been described as rape. The lads had paid their half-crown and wanted their money's worth.

It was like eight pints in pursuit of a Martini. When the band leader cried, 'Take your partners,' that, literally, is what happened. The women all yelled, 'I'm here with a friend,' but it was no use. In a flurry of pink tickets they were hauled off into the night, and the dawn saw whole platoons of men, weary with walk, dragging their limbs homewards, having made the mistake of choosing a partner who lived miles in the wrong direction.

I learned to dance as a result of one of these excursions. My friend landed me with the mother of his partner, and this brisk harridan dragged me about on a polished surface, calling me son, and messing up my shoes and drinking time. Thereafter, I applied for instruction to a man I knew who ran a dancing academy.

Here was no fading violet. He had the look of a man who could handle himself well against up to half a dozen others on a dark night. I demanded privacy for my lessons and this, a splendid instructor, said that it would all be utterly private. Figuratively, the lessons were all in a plain envelope. The first lesson, with his wife, was fine. During the second, she was called away unexpectedly, and I was left waltzing with her mate to the sound of a gramophone in a large, and otherwise deserted, ballroom. 'No,' he kept saying, 'you lead.'

So he persisted, and I persisted, and then his wife walked in and we were locked in musical harmony, gliding and kicking about all over the place. Eventually, they turned me out to the world, a graduate loosely proficient in the waltz, the quick-step and slow foxtrot. A close observer might even have noticed the difference in step and tempo between the various styles as I pursued my erratic path across the floor.

I immediately made my way, of course, to the Saturday night hop where I had been so often defeated in the past, and was asked to dance by a girl named Nellie. What with my new steps and her remarkable dexterity born of long sessions with other girls of her age and size, we did a circuit of the floor before anyone else had started, all her ten thousand sequins jingling and flashing, and her taffeta rustling. She was still going a bit strong when we fell on the third circuit and slid, gently, together, still jingling and jangling, to the very ramparts of the soft drinks counter, where the eight-pint mob were leering and sneering and mouthing obscenities through what remained of their teeth and the froth.

I was lethargic about dancing after that.

However, when my army days were over, a regiment was having its annual dance at the old hall. My friend, an ex-Welsh Guardsman, and myself went, not to dance, but to assert our new freedom as civilians, to repay the army, as it were, for having so diminished our egos in an uncomfortable relationship. We lounged about, hair draped like Spanish curtains, hands in pockets, eyeing the silverware, which was guarded by two privates with rifles.

'Is that necessary?' I said to a major. 'All that rifle stuff?'

'Certainly, sir,' he replied. 'That silver is priceless.'

'This is grand,' I said to my friend. 'We can get our own back for all that square-bashing.'

We afflicted a colonel, and he invited us for a drink. Then we chatted up the RSM, a fierce man, in a condescending manner. He called us sir, too, and we would like to have taken him home to keep in a cupboard for festive occasions. Then the colonel happened to walk by, unobserved by us but not by the sergeant-major, who bellowed *'sir'*. It was an awful noise, quite frightening. It awakened a thousand nightmares. It resounded in our heads. The RSM had flailed himself into a rigid, quivering symbol of discipline and obeisance. My friend and I behaved like Pavlovian rats. Or dogs. We reacted on impulse, as the army had taught us to react, and there we stood, the three of us, stiff as frozen socks, my friend and I unable to relax a muscle without being observed. The RSM took on a piggy look. He slapped his leg with his little stick very thoughtfully, and narrowed the eyes. He knew, and we knew, that our cover was blown: the dance was over for us, and we slunk out.

I applied myself, then, to learning a number of steps not in any book – fancy stuff where the eye had to be quick to keep pace with the feet. Armed with my new dexterity, I visited an expensive club in London. I tried out my steps and, sweating, looked around after five minutes to discover that my partner and I were the only ones left in action. The rest, stricken dumb by our performance, were standing in a half circle, eyes glazed, whether in admiration or horror, I will never know.

When I went, as a guest, to a posh Lancashire wedding, a number of London people were around looking like missionaries. They seemed a bit unsure about whether they would end up in the pot. I assured them that the North was as sophisticated as any other place; that tales of barbaric habits were fabrications; that their impressions of the region were formed purely from observing visitors doing vile things to their fountains on football days. They appeared convinced. We later went out into deep country, to a particularly good pub which had log fires and lots of oak beams. The visitors were totally at home. Then, in the distance, the sound of music; a dance at the village institute. Here, they thought, was an opportunity to observe our sophisticated ways. We all went, paid half a crown at the door, and had the backs of our hands stamped in thick blue ink in lieu of a ticket. If, thereafter, they wanted to visit the loo, the John, or whatever they wished to call it, they had to display their hands to an attendant. You could observe by the expression on their faces that it was not at all the sort of thing that happened at the Dorchester.

A dance band conductor announcing the next dance, to the tune of 'Granada': 'Ladies and gentlemen – Grandad.'

The Royal Liverpool Philharmonic Orchestra was assembled on a railway station platform when a goods train went by laden with vegetables. 'I see,' said a voice, 'that the Hallé is on tour as well.'

We were rehearsing the third act of *Falstaff*, which begins with a very lovely, delicate scene in Windsor Forest, and we had a full complement of wind and brass. The third trumpet was ill, so they brought me a local one, a Scot, and he was really – pooh! I had a very bad corn and conducted in a slipper and in the end I just let go at this poor chap. At the interval, I saw him advancing towards me. I thought: I'll face him in the cause of Verdi.

'Excuse me, sir,' he said, 'your feet are troubling you, aren't they?' I said, 'Very much so.' He said, 'Well, I'm not really a trumpet player. I'm a chiropodist.' He came to my hotel with a little box in which he had the most revolting collection of ingrowing toenails and other things he had extracted with great skill.

Sir John Barbirolli.

I remember the first time I went to London in 1967. There are people in my town who have never been to Manchester. My mother was working for a grocer and a woman there named Brenda. She said to me, 'You've got to be very careful in London.'

I said, 'What do you know about London? You've never been there.'

She said, 'You'll get your pockets picked. Brenda did. She's been in London has Brenda.'

I said, 'She only stopped at Victoria Station on her way back from a package holiday.'

She put the fear of God in my mother that I was going to have my pockets picked. She talked about rogues, thieves and vagabonds, all that kind of stuff – 'You look round and your luggage has gone.' Mother put me on a train. The ticket inspector came along between Leeds and London and I'm sitting there, a lovely girl opposite, and I'm trying to attract her attention, and having little fantasies about meeting her in London. I felt in my Burton director's suit, which cost twenty-two guineas – good shoes, too, you know – and I could not get my hand in my pocket. My mother had put a zip in with a flap over the zip and press studs all along the edge. True! The ticket inspector was standing there saying, 'Come on, lad, tickets, please,' his clippers champing away like the jaws of an animal. I was seventeen.

An opera singer.

An old man went to see the oratorio *Elijah* and was asked, jokingly, by a friend whether he had seen the prophet.

'Yes, I did.'

'What was he like, then?'

'Well, he stood there at t'back of t'crowd on t'platform and he kept rubbing a stick across his belly and he groaned and groaned and groaned and you could hear him all over t'place.'

He had assumed the player of double bass 'cello in the orchestra to be Elijah.

Lancashire Stories, *Frank Hird.*

1855: Johnson's New Theatre, in the vicinity of Ellison's Tenement, a portable booth, opened. For the first night, the programme opened with a drama, *The Jewess, or the Council of Constance,* and the second piece was entitled, *The Factory Girl of Manchester.* Between these two performances was a dance by Mr Murphy. On the second night was brought forward that new and splendid drama now playing in London to crowded houses, entitled *Woman and her Master.*

The cast included the names of no fewer than 19 artistes, and the characters varied from the aristocratic 'Lord Moretown' to the insignificant 'Bandy-legged Jem'. This performance was followed by a dance by Mrs Murphy, and the entertainment concluded with more drama, *Black-eyed Susan.* The stage manager was Mr H. Barnes, the artist Mr A. Conville, and the machinist, Mr Carter, and the prices charged were: boxes 1s., pit 6d., gallery 3d. According to the programme, other beautiful dramas were in preparation, including, *The Lonely Man of the Ocean* and *Ben Holt.* That order and decorum on stage were a matter of some importance was evident from the last line on the bill: 'No strangers will be allowed behind the scenes on any pretence whatever'.

Accrington Chronology and Men of Mark.

A young man, after a day's work, walked five miles and over two ranges of hills from Dean to Haslingden Grane to practise. At 2 a.m. the following morning, he ventured to say he thought that he should be going home. An enthusiastic old man, who also had several ranges of hills to cross on his way home, said reprovingly, 'If tha'rt allus i' such a hurry, tha'll never mek a musician as long as ever tha lives.'

From the diary of Moses Heap.

A tackler bought a piano for his girlfriend and one of his overlooker friends eventually asked, 'How's that girl getting on with it?'

'Grand,' replied the tackler. 'She's been on t'white keys up to t'present, but I don't think there'll be any harm now if she wants to start on t'black 'uns.'

A tackler who bought a piano was seen wheeling it, using a hand cart.

'Have you sold it?' asked a friend.

'No,' replied the tackler. 'I'm just off to t'music teacher to have my first lesson.'

In the Grane lives an old miser called Andrew Scholes, locally known as Old Andrew, and on Sunday his dwelling was visited by crowds of young people who wished to hear him play his fiddle. But unfortunately, he had not got it in tune. It appears that about a year ago, some wag advised him to boil it, so as to improve its tone, and since that time it has lost its charm.

Bury Times, 8 May 1875.

On Saturday last, a canary-singing competition came off at the house of Mr Henry Dewhurst, Warner's Arms. There were 15 birds entered and singing, on the whole, was very good. The judge's decision gave universal satisfaction. Winners for quality singing: 1. brass pan, W. Birtwistle, Rawtenstall; 2. copper kettle, H. Radcliffe, Rawtenstall; 3. metal teapot, W. Heys, Bacup. A gold hoop was given to the bird which sang the longest times of ten minutes allowed, which was won by Mr Robert Cooper, of Accrington, the bird singing 371 seconds. The audience was very large, many being unable to gain admission. [Lark singing was also a popular entertainment.]

The most devastating music critic seems to have been employed by the *Rossendale Free Press*, around 1888: 'Of course, Mr Fred Gordon sang well – he always does. He has an excellent voice and makes the most of it. But why, in the name of common sense, does he not get some new songs? We have not the least hesitation in assuring him that the public are getting quite tired of "Revenge" (ha! ha!) and "Down in the Deep".' And of the soloist at a later concert: 'a fair to middling tenor of the wheezing school.'

RESOLVED:
   That we have elastic bands for music.
   That Mr Tomkins and Mr Tomlinson be in charge of the Israelites crossing the Red Sea.
   That any alteration of any kind to the bandmaster be left to Mr F. Tattersall.
   That Gilbert and R. Entwistle see to boiling coffee and sandwiches.
   That Mr Bedford bring in the soprano at once.
   That Gilbert Tattersall go on solo cornet if he can see his way.

From the minute book of Helmshore Prize Band.

Mayor giving vote of thanks to Sir Malcolm Sargeant and symphony orchestra during their visit to his small town: 'And thank you, Sergeant Malcolm, for bringing your band here tonight.'

15

FULL STEAM BEHIND

You could always recognise the men whose wives had old-fashioned
mangles. Their shirts were full of half buttons.

Mickey Finn, Liverpool comedian.

HE YEAR IS 1970 and an old woman, bent like a safety pin,
pushes a truck full of washing. She says she can't stop, love,
because the old fellow will be home for his tea; but if you want her
opinion – not just her opinion but her *honest* opinion – about public
wash-houses, they are the best places in the world apart, that is, from
the danger of rheumatics.

The public wash-house she has just left, in Dainton Street, Ancoats,
Manchester, looks like an over-worked old tooth in a mouthful of
gum. Alone, it puffs and grunts in a wasteland where once there
were houses and schools and pubs. By the laws of progress, it should
be dead, but it thrives, steaming warmly, nurtured by people from
towns miles away.

Manchester and Liverpool have more wash-houses than the rest of
England combined at this time and they are still being built. Manchester, Liverpool and Glasgow are the high altars of wash-housery.
Sometimes the equipment is brand new: soap and soda injected
automatically, choice of twelve-pound or twenty-pound machines,
automatic spin drying, one ironing machine for every two customers,
complete drying tumblers for all, water like silk.

In others, the Amazons whirl the clothes in iron horses, red pipes
for hot, white pipes for cold. The front-loaders occasionally spew
white tides of soap to stroke the floor, a gorgeous sight to the women.

In an office where you buy your ticket, a coke fire burns and on the
mantelpiece is a first-aid box labelled ARP (for Air Raid Precautions),

a relic from a quarter of a century before. Wellington boots are everywhere. The women work like drudges. There is a constant procession of old prams and trucks, some passed on by women too old now to go to the wash-house, and here is the whitest white you will ever see, the boiled white right out of an advert.

Once, there were dolly tubs, possers, wringers – the word for wringer from the iron rings in the walls. Sheets were fed through them, then twisted to eject water.

The women they called 'professionals' spent much of their lives in the wash-houses making profit 'doing' for others. They were the ones with a tendency to suffer from rheumatism, so they say.

Women arrive in cars now. Rumour has it that a Rolls occasionally appears at a public wash-house like this in Manchester. Certainly, there are Rovers, many Minis. One woman arriving in a Mini says she does not like to go there in her beads and things, which might make her look toffee-nosed, so she changes into trousers at the office.

Wash-houses such as this were born in poor areas where people died unprotesting in their twenties. Legend has it that Kitty Wilkinson was founder: Kitty the Scouse, who gathered together some elementary things for carrying out a weekly wash in Liverpool and allowed the neighbours in. The first Baths and Wash-houses Act, allowing local authorities to build establishments, came later, in 1846. A penny for the first hour, threepence for two hours including drying. If the women did not pay, the corporation could keep the clothes …

From overcrowded areas, wash-houses and baths took their legions into a cleaner future, possers (an implement on a stick for pounding clothes in the tub) bright, rubbing boards erect. Everyone rediscovered what the Romans had tried to teach them all along with their public baths. The supervisor of Newton Heath Laundry and Baths says, 'You don't see much of the professional washers now. We used to get old people coming here at 7 a.m. and they would be in until 6 p.m. They were part of the place. They knew as much about a laundry as myself because they spent their lives in it. They would bring lunch and make a drink of tea, have their communal parties, tea and cakes; it was a part of their life.

'The job has altered because, at one time, you used to have what they called washing stalls. No machines, everything by hand – rubbing. When machines were introduced, a lot of the old-timers would not use them. It is all machines today. One time, if you pulled houses down in an area like this, the wash-house would lose trade, but that is not so today. We get schoolteachers, all sorts.'

A machine attendant at another wash-house says, 'A woman knows what she wants and she will get it. I do not think there is one in a thousand who can say they have gone home with a bad wash.'

The women are usually called ladies. One superintendent involved in a difference of opinion with a lady was suddenly propelled up the aisle by her mother, who had approached stealthily from behind. When a council decided to close a wash-house, more than a hundred chanting women waving banners marched on the town hall and dumped dirty washing on the steps. It surprised no-one.

One establishment had a machine you could hear miles away: a real clanker. It was very popular for that reason. The ladies invent their own names. Hydro-extractors are Whizzers.

Women shove thirty-five pounds of washing into a twenty-five-pounds machine and walk the clothes in prams looking like something out of a January sale. None has much time for your high-street laundromat. Some have the latest front-loaders at home, but they still go to the wash-house, where they get a good boil, then slot their sheets into drying cabinets, which have Sahara breath: 180°F when I tried it. Forty-five minutes for the washer, forty-five minutes for the dryer, the rest for machine-ironing. You book your machine and women will be faithful to a particular one. In the past, when customers grew old, they tried to pass on their places at the machines, as if they were legacies.

The ladies are fierce in defence of the old, mistrusting the new. There is nothing like a good boil. Mrs Catherine Stiles, mother of Manchester and England's footballer, Nobby, presented a 320-signature petition for the reprieve of one wash-house. She had been going there thirty years. Not uncommon.

The wash-houses, sixteen in Manchester, are subsidised by rates and are lively as ever, getting better year by year, they say. As the old woman declared, 'Rheumatics or not, it is the best five-and-sixpenceworth [27p]' in the world. But then, the year is 1970, and times have changed.

A tackler's wife asked him to oil a mangle while she was out shopping. An hour later, when she returned, he was exhausted.

'Have you oiled that mangle?' she said sharply.

'I have,' replied the tackler, 'and a terrible job it has been. Th'oil can were in our bedroom and I've had to drag t'mangle upstairs and back again.'

Conversation (true) between two women:
   'Well, is she out of hospital, then?'
   'Oh yes.'
   'How is she?'
   'Well, it will never be any use to her again – not as a leg, that is.'

> *Observed by Roy Barraclough, of Cissie and Ada*
> *(with Les Dawson) and Coronation Street.*

Fellow meets a friend he has not seen for two years and this conversation takes place ...
   'How are you getting on?'
   'Terrible.'
   'Still at the mill?'
   'No. I got caught pinching, got sacked.'
   'How's the wife?'
   'She died the other week.'
   'That's tough. How's your Frank getting on?'
   'Got killed in a car crash twelve months back.'
   'And the kids?'
   'All at foster homes.'
   'What are you doing for a living now?'
   'Selling lucky charms outside Lewis's.'

A group of men were on their way to work, arguing about whether they should actually start. One said, 'I'll chuck my cap up and if it comes down, we're not going.' He threw his cap into the air and railwayman leaning over a bridge above caught it. 'Now you'll have to go,' said the railwayman.

(True.)

Two tacklers walking to work on a frosty morning had to negotiate a downward slope three hundred yards long. One removed his clogs, saying, 'I'll walk in stockings so as to get a better grip on this ice.' His friend did likewise. When they reached level ground, the first tackler replaced his clogs.
   'Oh heck,' said his friend, 'I've left mine at t'top.'

Tackler to labourer: 'Why don't you put that shuttle where I told thi?'
'You never told me nowt.'
'Don't talk back to me.'
'I'm only telling thee.' (Tackler aims ball of string at labourer. Labourer ducks and the missile breaks a window.)
Tackler: 'Now look what you've done.'
'I did nowt. It were thee.'
'Get your cards. You're sacked.'
'What for? You broke t'window.'
'Get your cards. If you hadn't ducked, it wouldn't have broken.'

'Alice, we've been courting now for fifteen years. Don't you think it time we got wed?'
'Aye, but who'd have us?'

Two old men sitting on a bench outside a church on a Sunday morning.
'Bells are nice.'
'What?'
'Bells – they're nice.'
'It's no use, I can't hear thee for them blasted bells.'

A tackler's wife came home envious of a neighbour's decorating. 'Don't worry, lass,' said her husband. 'Get t'paper and I'll stick it on.' She got the wallpaper, handed it to the tackler, and went to her mother's. When she returned, he said, 'Well, how do you like it?'
'All right,' she said, 'but what are those lumps?'
'Dammit,' he said, 'I forgot to take t'pictures down.'

A couple had a pup which regularly misbehaved beneath the sofa.
'You'd better do something about it,' said the wife.
'Oh, I'll stop it, lass,' said her husband. When she returned from shopping, she found he had sawn off the sofa legs.

Albert Modley joke: There's a train coming down this track at eighty miles an hour, and another train coming down another track at eighty miles an hour and they are both heading for this single track. Railway-man in t'signal box looks outside and sees what is happening, and there's a fellow there in a wheelchair who likes to see trains going by. T'signalman dashes out, grabs t'wheelchair, pushes it to t'side of t'single track and says, 'Sit theer. Tha'll see t'best dam'd crash tha's ever seen in thi life.'

There was a big fire in Oldham, hoses everywhere. A fireman's helmet lay in the road. A coloured mill worker picked it up, put it on, and walked towards the flames.

'Where are you from?' asked the fire chief.

'Pakistan,' replied the worker.

'Good lord,' said the chief. 'They're not here from Manchester yet.'

Doris Thomson of Blackpool Pleasure Beach: 'We have a Noah's Ark, a very old device here in my father's time, and when TV became popular, an aerial was attached to it. One wet afternoon, an old couple complained that they had paid to go in the ark to see TV and there wasn't any. We apologised and gave them their money back.'

A weaver at an Oswaldtwistle mill lived some two hundred yards away from the premises. Going home for lunch, she found she had no key, so she went back to the mill to ask a tackler to get a ladder and climb through her upstairs window, and let her in. He did as she asked and opened the door for her, then leaned on the ladder and chatted for a while. Finally, he said, 'I'll be getting back, now,' whereupon he walked past her, went back upstairs, and climbed down the ladder.

Ancient joke past its sell-by date: A tackler going out on a Saturday night when the weather was unpleasant was given money by his wife to get a cab home. He arrived drenched. 'Why didn't you get a cab?' asked his wife.

'I did,' said the tackler. 'I sat up front wi't'driver.'

A tackler took his wife out for the night, returned home, put his car in the garage, then remembered what he had thus far forgotten: his wife.

Contributed anonymously 'because he is still living nearby.'

A tackler was asked to adjust a door which operated by means of a weight on a rope. The weight was touching the ground, so he dug a hole beneath it.

Herbert Bartlett talking about his love life in a pub: 'Well, I got into bed last night and she'd left a chink in t'curtain and there was a full moon. I looks at this full moon for a long time and, well, you know me – I mean, it's not like me – but I gives her a nudge and I says, "Hey, love, I feel like, you know?" – and she says, "Oh, all right, then. But you wakened me up. I was fast asleep." And later, I turns o'er and there's still that moon shining and I couldn't sleep for it. And after another hour or so, you'll never believe this, knowing me. I mean it's not that ...' 'We know it's not.' 'Well, you know, I felt just t'same again. So I gives her a nudge and I say, "I'm sorry to bother you, but I feel like it again." And do you know what she said? She said, "Oh bloody hell, Bartlett." '

True, names changed.

There's a fellow in t'pub with this dog, and he says, 'My dog will only do what I tell it.'

Another says, 'I bet ten shillings it will do what I tell it to do.'

'Never. You make that a pound if you like.'

'Done,' said the challenger, picking up the dog and throwing it on the fire.

'Now,' he said, 'geddoff.'

'Will you come in and shut that door, lad. That draught is cutting through me like a knife.'

'I can't. I'm looking at t'moon.'

'Looking at t'moon? Come in this minute and leave t'moon alone.'

'I'm not touching t'moon.'

When work was scarce, a parson met a man taking his dog for a walk. 'Do you think it right to keep that dog when your wife and children are half starving?' asked the cleric. 'It would be a great deal better if you sold the dog and bought a pig.'

'A bonny foo' I'd look going rabbiting wi' a pig,' said the man.

Adapted from Lancashire Stories, *Frank Hird.*

16

Everyone on cue

A N OLD BILLIARDS HALL is like a creature left on a beach when the tide has gone: it looks faintly helpless and squirms in its memories. In 1970, I found Cheetham Hill Temperance Billiards Hall in Manchester, a giant of a place in fact and memory, still thriving, shilling-a-year membership, and looking like the rear of Nelson's flagship – bow-windowed and slightly splendid. Inside, a drift of smoke, many shadows, sixteen tables, twenty people.

At midday, some pies are trapped in a plastic heater while a kettle interminably huffs and puffs on a gas ring. The roof is high-arched, half way between a railway station and a church, sixty years old. Everyone attracts a nickname: Double Vision, Lazzie, Big Sam, Wiggie, Boots, Pipky, Wolfy.

'That's the man they call Double Vision,' says the manager, Francis Logan, pointing. 'When he plays he asks for a big start because he says he has double vision. He pots the balls from all directions and opponents think *they've* got double vision. He's good, but the real good players could eat him.'

Well-meaning gentlemen built halls like this to keep the lads out of the pubs. The run of a ball over green often hooks them for life. A magnificent obsession.

Rendal Wilson, or Pipky, has known this place forty-five years now. He sits in repose within cue distance of a table recalling the time he played thirty-six hours non-stop, no sitting down. He lived on cups of tea and sandwiches.

'When we couldn't stand up any longer, we have had to go home and sleep, and we've come back again about twenty-four hours later and started again for twenty-four to thirty hours. You only notice time in thighs or arms. You don't feel sleepy. You begin to drag your feet. Only thing then is a good hot bath. Soak your limbs. Try to take the strain out.'

There is no climbing on the tables, no spitting and no foul language.

You get barred for that. Night-time, you ring the bell and get in if you are a member: 250–300 are.

Players come from Liverpool, Leeds, all over the place, and the hunger is money, often good money. Hustlers, good players touring halls pretending to be mugs, get short shrift. They usually find themselves against a player who beats them.

'I don't encourage people to lounge all day,' says the manager, who is known as Michael, not Francis. 'If they stop for a few hours and they don't play I ask them to leave. Prior to starting this twenty-four-hour business, we had a load of bums coming and sitting and not playing. A shilling-a-year membership was a cheap home. It's a very hazardous business with staff. You might get the odd rough character trying to get in.'

'We've had some characters in here,' says Rendal Wilson, *alias* Pipky. 'I had one from Sheffield. I said, "I only play for what I can get out of it. I don't like playing for the novelty." "Half a crown a game," he says, "colours only." I thought: That suits me – four games is ten bob and all over in ten minutes. I finished £59 in front and I did not know him from Adam and Eve. He wrote a cheque – Barclays Bank, Sheffield. I was on the express train next morning to Sheffield. When the bank opened I was there. Cashed the cheque, no trouble. I was back in the hall here at twenty past one and he was waiting.

'He says, "Are we having another game?" Same half crown. That went on for a long time and he always paid by cheque. I thought to myself: This fellow must be SFH.'

'Soft in the head?'

'No, sent from heaven. I thought: It's a shame to keep beating him, so I lost eleven games on the run on purpose. He was tickled pink and I paid him eleven half crowns. It was the only time he won. I went to his house, a very big house, one Sunday in Sheffield and his son was riding about on a horse. "Come in," he says, "and meet the wife." He says, "I've lost money, tons of it, to fellows in the golf club and we were all bad snooker players, but I've improved, haven't I? You've no need to worry about the money I've been losing to you because I've had that back over and over again."

'Next time he comes down he says, "I'm moving to Stockport so I'll be nearer to you." I thought: This is lovely. I'll have him for ever. But when he went to Stockport I never saw him again.'

Monday and Friday good nights; Sunday a cracker. The manager closed one day for stock-taking but so many people rang the bell, he opened up again. Snooker never sleeps.

'We had a fellow used to play for 3*d*. a game,' says Rendal Wilson, 'and if he could win he was the happiest man in town. Married a girl with businesses and played then for big money. He won £8,000 on the pools, then another £4,000. I got him one day at the table and won £100. He lost £50 in side bets. The days he wasn't playing snooker, he was going to the dog tracks.

'He finished up losing the money and sweeping up. Yet he was always laughing. To this very day he laughs. Happiest man in the world. An ordinary man would throw himself in the river.

'I remember a chap coming in with a broken lighter. He says to one man, "If you buy this, Solly, I'll play you for what it's worth. Give us half a quid." So they played and Solly lost £22, all his money. Solly said, "I can't go home with no money. Buy the lighter back for ten bob." The man who'd sold it said, "It's not worth ten bob. I wouldn't give you a shilling for it." '

Not long ago, Rendal had played eighteen hours non-stop.

'My biggest break was eighty-eight about twenty-five years ago. There were sixteen halls built like this. There were eight billiards halls in Reading and me and my friend went there and there weren't any left. I reckon on about twenty to thirty hours a week [in the hall] on average.

'Not long ago I was asked to play and I refused. I had been off colour for about a fortnight. There are times when the game can send you off colour. You get sick of it. That's the time to rest. That's what I think after forty-five years of it ...'

17

A JUNGLE OF HURT

A professional cricketer long ago toured America and returned to face the wonderment of his friends. 'What was it like?'

'Oh, all right, I suppose.'

'But wasn't it exciting?'

'Not really.'

'But you must have seen some gradely things.'

'Happen.'

'Did you see Niagara Falls?'

'Yes, I did.'

'That must have been exciting. It is one of the wonders of the world – all that water tumbling down.'

The cricketer pondered the comment, then said, 'Well, so far as I could see, there were nowt to stop it.'

SUMMER WHISPERS TO LIFE the game of cricket, and some would have you believe that cricket is a languid game. Those who play it know otherwise; they know that it is a jungle of hurt played out in apparent innocence, never more so than in the Lancashire League. It brings out the best and worst in men. What spectators see is the graceful flowing of a white tide, an innocence, a pristine tableau, the untruth. Their comments mirror this tableau – 'Well played, sir', or, 'Good show, sir'.

If cricket were merely a good show, sir, it would be dead. The thing that keeps it beautifully alive, and makes it splendidly complex, is deviousness, or malice, or even, on occasion, hate.

If you know cricket, you know life, all of life, with hurt and torment, joy and exhilaration, pride, prejudice. You know philosophy, too. Football is the national sport. Cricket is the national character. Football measures skill and exposes weaknesses, but for me, at any rate, it is body without soul. Cricket, alone, is all-encompassing. I know of no greater stimulus than the smell, sight and sound of a pavilion opened up for the first time at the end of winter: smell of oil and musty fabric; sight of grown men, long dead, pictured on the walls with their austere beards and ludicrous schoolboy caps; sounds of spikes on wood. Generations have crunched their way to the wicket and then their graves. Here, the true freemasonry of men. ('Is that thine?' said a Yorkshireman at a Roses game, referring to the wife of the man in front of him, who had made one naive comment too many. Having an affirmative answer, he said, 'Well, tek t'bugger hooam.')

Having said all that I admit myself a fake, or at least someone running on the reputations of others. I played in the Lancashire League at the age of sixteen which appears, at first sight, an achievement of minor note. The truth is otherwise. We had in our team League notables such as Fred Hartley, Reg Parkin (son of Cecil) and Tommy Lowe snr. For that reason the team did not need me, though it was considerate enough to give me a silver teapot recording the fact that it (rather than me) had won the league championship. I batted around number five and the opposition rarely got past three. I spent so many hours in the outfield studying nature that I became a better horticulturist than a player. I knew the petals of a daisy rather more intimately than I did the position of third man.

I had, in short, time to ponder the beauty of the game. Sir Neville Cardus (in the *Manchester Guardian*) had already turned it into prose-poetry. One could read his words and hear birds singing. Others recorded the progression of fact – numbers of overs, scoring rate and so on, the chartered accountants of the game. He charted the beauties of weather and play and movement. He soared to sublime heights. On occasion, too sublime. A friend who studied old records once phoned him and said, 'Neville, this description of yours [referring to a key moment in a county game]; beautiful, but from my records, I can not for the life of me see how you could have been there.'

'Well,' said Cardus after a long pause, 'it *felt* as if I'd been there.'

I began to see subtleties and grasp the ethos long before I met Cardus. The truths involved this jungle of hurt – delicious hurt – to which I have referred. There is the hurt one imposes on a batsman. As a bowler, one seeks out his weaknesses and if all else fails, one fells him. I saw Constantine fell a batsman on a League ground and no-one ever called him anything other than a sportsman of the highest integrity. He did it, so far as I am concerned, quite deliberately as the final solution to a problem which, at the time, seemed insoluble by any other means. He is not diminished in my mind because of it. He merely pursued the inevitable. He caused the ball to hit a batsman three times in one over: no undue reticence there, either.

Stumpers, more than batsmen, always provoked me. The sight of them, crouching like old frogs and even, occasionally, croaking like old frogs, caused me, early on, to lengthen my bowling run to thirty-two yards. I liked to see them fretting and leaping about, complaining when the ball thudded into their tender parts. I was learning. I discussed this with a friend who once saw Len Hutton hit similarly. Hutton, he says, danced all round the wicket massaging his injuries, eyes watering, and in the silence a spectator cried, 'Stop pleasurin' thissen and get on wi't'game.'

I came across a chap who says he was stumper in my last game, many years ago. He stood fifteen yards back because he became disturbed by the length of my run. He had reason to be disturbed. He was unprotected at his most vulnerable point, boxless. In attempting to avoid the ball, he was struck in this boxless area by the middle stump and declared immediately that he would never play again. So we retired together, he crouched low as if carrying a heavy load and I, at least, satisfied that my last recorded act should be so satisfying in its conclusion.

It is the curious mixture of impeccable conduct and sadism which makes the game what it is. Punishment and deviousness are essential ingredients. Bowling with flapping sleeves is, and always has been, unfair, since the batsman can confuse ball with sleeve, but you get away with it if you can. It is expected, and always has been expected of any bowler, that he should pitch the ball into the sun, or into any convenient shadow. Few ploys are unacceptable so long as they are subtle, though a batsman who regularly presented his rear to the bowler (since he could think of no other way of saving his wicket) was told by the umpire, 'Jack, that ain't cricket. When a man stops a ball with *that*, he must be out.'

A chap named Fitzgerald, who wrote *Jerks in from Short Leg* said, poker-faced, that the captain should choose the fattest man for point, 'for nature makes it impossible for him to get out of the way of a hard hit.' He knew his cricket. How curious that the game should produce both W. G. Grace ('Temperance in food and drink, regular sleep and exercise' as the requirements of a batsman) and an umpire who, when asked why he had not give a baronet out, declared, 'Lor' bless you, sir, I've been his valet for fifteen years and I dussn't. He gets awful wild at times.'

The sum of such contradictions is the mystic agreement we all recognise. When we propelled lads into nettles at Church cricket club for not abiding by our rules, we were carrying on a long English tradition. I first realised the pain of the game when I faced a huge professional named Warburton in the Lancashire League. He bowled like a missile launcher. I was 108½ pounds in weight, pale, and just gone sixteen. I expected, therefore, that he would introduce into his bowling a delicacy of delivery to match my frame and status. He did not. He increased his thirty-yard run by so great a distance that I assumed he was going home.

Men harbour their best recollections of cricket like women harbour their romanticisms. I saw Eddie Paynter (Lancashire and England) fielding on a boundary and the ball arced towards him from an area of the sky where only skylarks are to be found; and instead of waiting for it, teetering and anxious, he bent down, plucked a long blade of grass, stuck it between his teeth, looked up at the right moment, and caught the ball as precisely as most players would have done had they merely been passing it from one hand to the other.

Such moments establish one's strongest memories in the long time of cricket, and they can be recounted in county pavilions as if one had presented credentials. They are the badge of being and authority.

Once, in the Lancashire League, on a Whit Monday, six thousand saw an Enfield match at Accrington, and afterwards '1,500 young people tripped the light fantastic to the strains of the Enfield Old Original Brass Band.' That was before my time. But within my memory, Constantine and Headley and Amar Singh and Amar Nath and Martindale and Miller came among us from parts of the world many of us could hardly comprehend at the time. They came with style and grace that hushed us to a kind of reverence. We tried as best we could to be like them, but somehow our efforts were not like theirs. One Fred Stubbins, after suffering a bout of my vicious bowling, once chased me into the hawthorn bushes with a wildly-flailing stump. It carved a furrow in my eyebrow. I bear a slight mark to this day. We expected that kind of thing. We imagined it took place at the Oval. The flame was fierce.

Great characters had preceded me. There was a stumper named Ralph Coupe who regularly inserted one raw steak in each glove before every game. He protected his hands like a woman protecting her child. See him set there, like stone, rump projected, ten yards back to a fast bouncer, flicking out a glove that plopped richly with impact, sure and steady. See the crowd nod its approval. Hear the whisper, 'Ralph has got his steak in today.' And then the miracle when, fully protected, infinitely experienced, ever watchful, he took a rising ball which screwdrivered the edge of one hand. 'He's down,' they cried, and indeed, he was, threshing about with the stricken expression of the man who discovered the earth was round must have had. The impossible had happened. Ralph had broken his thumb. 'Man,' as one observer put it, 'can not live by steak alone.' He preceded me, as did a couple of notable players, one of whom was deaf, the other earnest. No. 1 would stroke the ball away with a flick of the bat and shout, 'Yes!' No. 2 would be lost in his own thoughts, static. No. 1, all arms, would project himself at speed. No. 2, motionless, would come to with a start at the rush of wind and leap forward. No. 1, by this time mortified, would change his mind and begin the complicated process of putting himself in reverse. And the two of them would finally head towards the same wicket.

On one occasion, when they did start from opposite ends at the same time, they did so with such zeal that they collided head on in the centre, and there was such a bellowing and stumbling and a rubbing and a wailing that the opposing team was rendered static by emotion. One old player became an umpire and took a brilliant catch at square leg.

When, long ago, I made a pilgrimage to Church to see the old wooden pavilion, it had vanished, and there's a pity. It had style and maturity: home team to the left, visitors to the right, a big clock always in danger of destruction surmounting the whole. I had died in there and been re-born and now all that existed was a bare patch. The teams were housed in what looked like a couple of converted ice-cream kiosks and I concluded that they must undress each other.

I could not find the big roller. A horse used to pull it and make more marks in the pitch than the roller took out, so they got rid of the animal and used the free labour of men instead. Then they got a motor roller and I ran it through the First XI nets while Tom Clapperton, the groundsman, hopped and screeched.

Tom hated the old men who lined up during the week to lean on their sticks and criticise what he was doing. 'Missed a bit there, Tom,' they would say, prodding the grass. If you could hit an old man's kneecap with the ball at fifty yards, you were a hero. If they saw a ball approaching from a great height, they used to shove each other around in the hope that it would hit someone else.

An unlikely notice had appeared: 'No dogs allowed on the ground except during matches'.

It is not a notice I recalled from the time when, as a right-handed batsman, I wore a pad on the left leg from April through September. Dogs never sat in rows, watching us. Flat caps did; and loud voices emerged from beneath them, proving them to be occupied. On the whole they were kind to me if only because I was the youngest player. The older players took a lot of stick. 'Get a bucket, Ducket!'

They had wooden flooring in the grandstand then and pennies slid through to the soft earth beneath. Sunday morning was always a good time to go hunting for money down there among spiders in the gloom. Grown men might be out of form at various parts of the season, but they perked up when it neared their holidays. Their bats flashed like rapiers in pursuit of collections. I got very few of those myself, but spent a long time walking round the ground jingling a few coppers in a wooden box and shouting 'Sam Pilkington, fifty please.' The sight of a wooden table filled with pennies and the odd sixpence was wondrous indeed to one who had to root for them under a grandstand. I often wondered how the players carried them home.

A barrage balloon used to soar silver in the sky above all this and deposit ice at your feet in July.

We should be glad, I suppose, that we can now push a button in our own homes and watch Test matches, the great players instantly available in living light, performing on table tops like glove puppets.

Lancashire League batsman Jimmy Brierley used to open the batting with the professional, whom he ran out twice in succession.

'Jimmy,' said the captain, 'the pro isn't happy opening with you.'

'That's all right,' said Brierley, 'I'll take somebody else in with me, then.'

In a Lancashire–Yorkshire game at Sheffield, Walter Brearley, from Bolton, fast bowler for Lancashire, said, 'Ah hit George Hirst bang on t'kneecap and Ah'll swear to my dyin' day he was in front: t'ball would have knocked all three stumps down. But t'umpire gives it not out and then George hits me over t'ropes and t'crowd shouts, 'Ow's that, Maister Brearley?' And next ball, he hits me again over t'ropes and t'crowd shouts, 'Ow's that?' again. So I knocks his middle stump flying and in two, and Ah runs down t'pitch and picks up t'broken halves and Ah shakes 'em at t'crowd, and then Ah runs off t'field and comes back wi' six new stumps and gives 'em to t'umpire and says, 'Here, tek these, you'll need all t'bloody lot before Ah've done.' And he needed four on 'em, Ah can tell you.

Sir Neville Cardus (who married in June 1921 during a Lancashire innings and returned to find that the score had increased by seventeen in his absence), talking to me at his London home.

A team of tacklers challenged a team of weavers to a football match, winners to pay for supper. The weavers were short of a goalkeeper, so the tacklers suggested they have old Jim, a huge man capable, it seemed, of letting nothing past him. The tacklers scored seven, weavers nil. So old Jim was severely criticised afterwards.

'Why,' his side asked, 'did you not stop 'em?'

'Stop 'em?' he said. 'I thought that was what I hadn't to do. What's t'net for?'

Knowing nothing about racing, two tacklers went to a racecourse for the first time in their lives, and after studying the race card for some time, one said, 'Let's have a shilling on t'four o'clock race, and we'll back t'horse that wins t'Trial Stakes at 3.30. It can't be far off winning if it comes in first in a trial.'

A tackler was watching a game of tennis and decided it was the game for him. So he went to an outfitter and asked to see a selection of rackets. He was disappointed by what he saw. 'That's no good to me,' he said to the assistant. 'I want a proper racket, one with a pair of white boots on.'

Long ago, journalists used to send reports to an evening newspaper by pigeon. A correspondent who took three pigeons with him to Ewood Park, Blackburn Rovers' ground, successfully launched two with accounts of the game tied to their legs. A goal was scored in the final moments. In his excitement, he grabbed the third pigeon, shouted the result in its ear, then launched it. 'God dammit,' he said, as the bird vanished over the horizon.

18

THE EDDIE AND RAY SHOW

IN THE SUMMER OF 1981, the world of Rugby League shook:
Eddie Waring, the BBC commentator, whose vowels always came
strangulated from the throat as if equipped with tiny clogs, gave way
to a new voice; that of Ray French, a teacher and storyteller, then
forty-one years of age, six foot three inches, a native of what Waring
would have called Sentellins (St Helens) and with a nose pointing in
a direction slightly at variance with that of his face – the honourable
result of various rugby conflicts. This is how he splendidly described
to me facts of the most bruising of Northern pastimes and his part
in them:

'I remember at Widnes, we signed up a new Rugby Union player,
and it was in the BBC2 floodlit. No-one had met him beforehand at all;
and he was due to arrive at seven o'clock. He arrived late, about ten
past, and we were kicking off at half past. Huge character. I'll not tell
you his name. He took size twelve boots. In a Rugby League dressing
room you don't have many. The biggest pair we had there that night
was size ten. The only suggestion anybody could give him was that
he put these boots on without the laces and the skip man had this
wonderful idea that if he stood in a bucket of water, it would soften
these boots up and mould on his feet. Then he could lace them up.

'At twenty-five past seven, there's this new forward having his first
game in Rugby League in his life, his feet in a bucket of water,
wearing boots with no laces, and the referee's coming in to check
players' studs. Anyway, we actually got him laced up and we went
out, and the idea was that in the first twenty minutes I, as captain,
would just give him a few balls, give him a run, send him through,
get him into the game, and I did do that. After all that, I could not
find him anywhere on the field. Where the hell's he gone? I thought.
He was about thirty yards behind play, on the floor. I thought he
was injured. I went back to him and said, "What's up?" He says,
"It's me boots – they've shrunk. I can't move. What are we going to

do?" I said, "Well, look, I'll bring play towards you and then just go down. Clutch the back of your leg as if you have a hamstring or something." So this is what we did. He went down and his feet were blue. Couldn't move his legs. They had to lift him to get him off. It was the time when BBC used to come on with the game at 10.30 – they recorded it – and you could watch the match in the club house. And there he was, being carried off, and Eddie Waring was saying, "That's a very bad hamstring injury." He couldn't move because of these boots. They got him some twelve-and-a-halfs for the following week. Don't find out his name for God's sake ...

'Took a school team to South America. My own school. We were sitting in the waiting room at Buenos Aires and the aircraft call came and, being a teacher, you always look for property left behind. There was this small carpet, about four feet by three, rolled up. The lads had been buying sheepskin stuff and I thought: Somebody must have bought this. It was also the time of all the hijacks. So I carted it through and I suddenly thought: Who would buy a carpet? Suppose there's a bomb in it. Supposing somebody's planted this. Better get rid of it. So I said to one of my prop forwards, "Get rid of this." He said, "Why?" I said, "I don't know whose it is." Anyway, we got on the plane, sat down, took off, and I looked up and there, above my head, is this carpet. It might sound daft, but you know how things build up in your mind. It was only a short leg. We were flying from Buenos Aires to Sao Paulo in Brazil to change planes, and I thought: That's a bomb. I was sweating. I thought: I'll look a fool if I tell anybody. When we landed, I got it down on the tarmac and undid the string around it, rolled it out and it was a gold carpet. There, in the middle, was the lettering: Buenos Aires Transit Lounge.'

Eddie Waring during a BBC commentary: 'That's either his head or the ball. We'll know when he gets up.'

Soccer

The most vitriolic football manager in Britain, certainly one of the best, a demi-god to his fans, a Victorian-style father figure to players, an awesome man full of menace to well-meaning amateurs who intruded on the game to which he dedicated his life and strength: such was Bill Shankly, manager of Liverpool FC. Strictly speaking, his humour, much of it unintended, should not be recorded here, because he was a Scot; but he adopted Lancashire to such an extent that he deserves special status, like Modley. What follows are Shankly-isms gathered by me both from him and those around him at the height of his career.

'I'd like to be healthy when I die.'

To a radio reporter, on air, who put an embarrassing question to him before a big game: 'You've been drinking, haven't you, son?'

Tannoying the crowd at Carlisle: 'This is your manager speaking. There is a report in the paper that Peter Doherty won't be playing and he's injured. I've just been to the dressing room and he's getting stripped. That's the fellow [indicating a reporter in the Press box] sitting out there, and I'll tell you another thing – he hasn't paid to get in.'

'Alec Lindsay [Liverpool] was a boy loaded with ability that was being thrown away. He was insulted, pushed, knocked about here, and he stuck it, kept his temper. Sometimes, if he had gone and shot me he would have been justified. I concentrated on him and tried to break his spirit by making him angry and maybe making him kick somebody. Then when he did kick somebody, it was a foul on the fringe of the box, and the other side scored and it lost us the game.'

A fellow player talking of a practice game: 'Once, when he got us all sparked up, Bill's going through with the ball and he's got us all rattled, and a player comes and jumps on his back. Bill just saw the open goal and carried on. He had to put the ball into that net before he did anything else.'

Shankly to player in pre-Liverpool days: 'Are you doing anything this afternoon? If you're not, come down to the ground.' They would then upturn two chimney pots on ashes in front of club buildings and play one-a-side football.

To a radio interviewer: 'Your questions are getting more and more amateurish, son.'

To Tom Finney (Preston) when their team was losing 4–1 and there were a couple of minutes left: 'Come on, come on, we haven't lost yet.'

'My conception of coaching is the right conception. Not fancy bloody carry-ons. I was lucky to be at Preston where they trained to play football. They didn't train to be marathon runners.'

Shankly arriving in New York. A member of the playing staff, knowing his liking for boxing, asks: 'Wouldn't you like to go to Jack Dempsey's bar?'

'But it's half past eleven at night.'

'No, there's a big time difference here.'

Shankly: 'It's half past eleven in Liverpool and I'm going to bed.'

'When I spoke to Liverpool Supporters' Club, it was like Churchill speaking to the nation.'

'Was it a good speech?'

'I don't know. I never heard it. I was too busy speaking. Speaking and listening are two different things.'

I love people. I support Rochdale and we got a black winger. One night, some of the bulbs had gone in our spotlights and we ended with a dark corner. Players were kicking hell out of this player, Whelan, because he was so tricky and this owd wag shouts, 'Get in this corner where it's dark – they'll not si' thi.' True as God's my judge.

Dudley Doolittle, comedian.

Bull-baiting at Haslingden: The bull was brought from the Bull's Head and tied to a stake in a meadow near Lower Lane. Dogs were then set upon it and the one which first pinned itself to the animal's nose gained the prize. (There was also a building where, for a shilling, 'the audience had the privilege of watching dogs tear each other to pieces.')

So firm a hold has the gambling mania got that when there are no other means of outlet, little knots of people gather ... near the railway line to lay odds or evens on the number of carriages an incoming train will consist of.

Haslingden Guardian, *19 January 1895, reporting 'astounding numbers of people betting in public places.'*

A Haslingden man, in a letter to the *Blackburn Standard* of 27 June 1855, suggested an augmentation of the local police force and complained: 'It really is disgraceful to see, Sabbath after Sabbath, groups of young men, unwashed, unshaved, and dressed in their everyday attire, standing at the corners of public streets flying pigeons, smoking, swearing, and from whose mouths proceed the most vile and beastly conversation, to the great annoyance and utter disgust of those

worshippers who are passing to and from their places of worship ...
It is only about a fortnight ago, and on a Sabbath day morning, when
a considerable number of these idle stragglers and scum of society
assembled about a mile out of town to witness a jumping match,
afterwards a foot race and, by way of a finish, resorted to the public
house to drink and talk over the merits or demerits of the several
competitors.'

John Barnes and Ralph Schofield were each fined 3s. 4d. at Haslingden
for wrestling for a wager of five shillings in Oswaldtwistle on the
previous Sunday. The defendants were in a state of nudity with the
exception of their stockings.

Bury Times, 11 June 1859.

A man named Ralph Holden of Haslingden Grane carried a stone 6 ft 3 ins in length 3 ft 1 in. in breadth and five-and-a-quarter inches thick on his back about two yards in the presence of a number of witnesses, although it had taken eight men to adjust it for carriage. The stone weighed a little over 13 cwt.

Blackburn Mail, 8 May 1824.

A cat race is the latest oddity in Haslingden sporting circles. Two well-known characters, about a fortnight ago, determined to test the locomotive skill of their respective 'mousers'. A prodigal stake of £2 a side was placed in the hands of a third party and the cats were conveyed in a basket to the starting point, a field behind the church at Edenfield. On being set free, the cats made for home in the direction of Irwell Vale. It then dawned upon the owners and handicapper, for the first time, that they had not made any arrangements at the other end for recording the arrival of the contestants.

The three men then took to their heels and reached home three miles distant utterly exhausted in something less than 30 minutes. They were relieved to find themselves in time. The cats had not yet landed. And they decided to keep a vigilant watch until the consignments of cat meat came to hand. They kept watch until five o'clock the following morning, but still the cats had not landed, and they retired to bed disheartened.

Days passed without anything being heard of the domestic truants and the backers had grown somewhat reconciled and would not have cared so much about this if the joke had not leaked out and the street arabs taken to yelling after them, 'Hey, has t'cats come home?' One of the backers, however, maintained unshaken confidence in his cat and was ultimately found to be correct, for at four o'clock on Wednesday morning, his feline competitor mewed a plaintive entreaty at the back door to be admitted. Generally speaking a cat has great endurance. As proof of this, the one in question made the journey from Edenfield to Haslingden in less than 11 days, ten hours, 45 minutes and some odd seconds and showed not the least signs of fatigue.

Rossendale Free Press, 12 February 1887.

19

AS SHE IS SPOKE

'That door,' said an East Lancashire friend of mine to his wife, 'is keykin.' ('Key' pronounced as in 'hey'.)

'What do you mean?' she asked.

'Keykin' o'er,' he said. 'Leaning.'

*D*IALECT IS A LITTLE LIKE SEX USED TO BE: a profound mystery; something that is always around but which, for many people, is not to be talked about. It is subject to bizarre laws. For the late Eddie Waring, dialect contributed to his success. Little Southern ladies were in awe of him as he treated his Rugby League commentaries to such picturesque embellishments as, 'It's a coat colder on the east coast.'

But for most Northerners accent is something they might retain as a luxury if they stay put, but which they must discard if they are to have credence in a wider world.

Of course there are many preservers of dialect around. They publish magazines and pamphlets and can quote verbatim such writers as Edwin Waugh (1817–90), Sam Fitton, Sam Laycock. But it is their pastime, their hobby. Like collecting antiques. Dialect writers are sentimentalist by nature rather than campaigners, concerned with effects rather than causes. They speak more of poverty than they do of its injustice. Fame, for the dialect writer, is confined. Riches are not to be had. He is like a dialect comic (Albert Modley, Frank Randle): he operates, often brilliantly, but in a confined space. If he is exceptionally good at what he does, he achieves this restricted immortality. All else is denied him.

Waugh is the man most quoted, the daddy of the dialect, and he was well aware of his restrictions. 'There is,' he wrote, 'as much difference in the tone of manners and language in the North and South as there is between the tones of an organ and those of a piano.'

Shame! Because much wisdom, and acute observation, is thereby confined within closed boundaries.

I came across these examples of folk observation in *Dunshaw, A Lancashire Background*, by T. W. Pateman, published in 1948:

> An old man from the country asked why he could not settle in a street: 'A pewit doesn'd nest in a downspout.'

> A widow receiving the condolences of a clergyman by the graveside: 'Aye, it's awreight thee talkin', but when all's said as con be said there's thirty-five shillin' a week lyin' down theer.'

> An old farmer seeing Furness Abbey for the first time: 'So that's wheer th'owd monks used to skulk their time away.'

> A youth, asked how he managed to get two girls pregnant, several miles apart, at the same time: 'You see, ah've getten a bike.'

As an example of a Northerner in full and glorious flood, I offer Fred Dibnah, Bolton steeplejack, great storyteller, splendid character, describing to me a Land Rover which he bought secondhand in 1969:

'It was a 1963 machine, ex-WD, four hundred and twenty-five quid, and we never had t'top off t'bloody engine and once we ran it for six months without oil. It is an interesting tale, like, because it makes a funny noise, an ex-army 'un, when it wants a drink of oil: a burbling sort of sound. I asked Crook Brothers, who sold it to me, what it were and he said it is summat to do with, you know, an oil-cooling thing or summat on t'front. Normal ones, they don't have it, like.

'Anyway, the thing is, this noise appeared, and you put two pints of oil down t'pipe, like, and it disappears, and a month later it will come back again, this noise. You have no need to work to any clocks. It is dead handy. Anyway, this bloody noise, it must have come and we didn't do anything about it and it gives up t'ghost after a bit. There's only one hill between here and Bury. Fired it up in t'morning and a hell of a racket it was, like a diesel, and as soon as it were on t'road, it were all right but up a slope, groaning like buggery.

'Anyway, I get a big wooden hut on wheels out of my garden, hell of a weight, about two tons, and I'm dragging it up t'hill with t'Land Rover, four-wheel drive, bottom gear – what a racket. And this bloke arrived and he said, "I always thought it was a petrol one, Fred, not a diesel." And I said, "It is a bloody petrol one," and he said, "Bloody big ends are going to come through t'side – it's knackered." Anyway, I thought it's served me well all these years. I'd never maintained it nor nothing. So I rings my mate up who has t'garage and I said, "Hey, John, what's crank shaft and bearings cost?" "Oh," he says, "don't bother with that. I'll get you a new engine." So the morning after, I looked at it and I don't know what made me do it, but I pulled t'dipstick and it were just like chromium plate, no signs of oil anywhere. I put two pints of oil in and put t'stick back in and it wasn't even touching t'stick. So I put another two in and it were just touching t'bottom of t'stick. So I put a gallon in and it were at t'right mark on t'stick. Pressed a button and it run sweet as a bloody nut. You'd never believe it. It must have been running literally with just a bare splash goin' on t'bearings. And it's twice as good as that lightweight vehicle I got. That bloody thing: I think they dropped it out of an aeroplane from forty thousand feet and it didn't land reight.'

20

THE WORK ETHIC

*J*UST BEYOND THE CHURCHYARD GATE, with its grim boundary wall, the old Thorn Inn flanks a long row of seventeenth-century tenements, one with a huge crooked beam embedded for no apparent reason in its rough, rubble masonry. They were typical of their period, and when tenanted by a local clan of handloom weavers, must have been a little hive of industry. But this fine old cottage craft ultimately fell upon evil times, and in 1841, when it was in its death throes, it was computed that for weaving a piece of cloth 40 inches wide and one mile in length, a handloom weaver received the sum of 33s. (£1.65). For this, his feet travelled on the treadle through a space of 900 miles; his hand, in picking the shuttle, travelled through a space of 2,160 miles. In addition, the weaver often travelled ten miles to and from the warehouse in delivering the finished pieces.

George C. Millar, A History of the Parish of St James, *Church Kirk, Church, near Accrington.*

A mob, not entirely composed of textile workers, smashed up machinery and buildings belonging to Richard Arkwright, near Chorley, in 1779. This really great man is said to have offered to finance the government of the day in their wars provided they would continue to him his patent rights for a number of years.

The Spinning Mule, *an account of the life of its inventor, Samuel Crompton, 1753–1827, published by Bolton Borough Arts Department.*

(Arkwright was once a Bolton barber. A peer said to him, 'Is it true, Sir Richard, that you were once a barber?' and Arkwright replied, 'Yes, and if you had begun life as a barber, my lord, you would have been one still.')

28 October, 1794 – By this indenture, I bind myself to pay unto Matthew Fawkner of Styal, the sum of five pounds eleven shillings upon demand and also assign over my household goods under-

mentioned unto the aforesaid Matthew Fawkner till the aforesaid sum of five pounds eleven shillings is paid and also allow him to sell them or any part of them for the payment of the aforesaid money and all expenses attending such sale of my goods:

One chest, 14s. One iron pot, 2s. One clock, 21s. One bed stocks, 9s. Seven chairs, 12s. A pair of bed stocks, 2s. 6d. Iron and heater, 5s. 6d. One map, 1s. 8d. Table, 6s. Grate and tongs, 11s. 6d. Frying pan, 1s. 4d. Bedclothes, 28s. Fork, 1s. 11d. Spade, 1s. 4d. Shuffill [shovel], 1s. Hatchat [hatchet], 2s. Mugs, 2s. 6d. Tin kettels, potts and mugs, 2s. 6d. Cupboard, 8s. Little stand, 1s. 9d. Sheets, 8s. Blankets, 10s. Copper kettel, 2s. 6d.

From The Family Economy of the Working Classes in the Cotton Industry *(Chetham Society, 1965).*

On the 19th ult. died, raving, in consequence of the bite of a mad dog – Webb, a butler in the service of Mrs Parker, of Cuerden, near Chorley. He was bit in July in his hand and leg. The symptoms of hydrophobia did not take place till within four days of his death. He made unusual noises in his convulsive exertions, but his physician says that the sounds of what he uttered did not resemble barking.

Blackburn Mail, *October 1795.*

By Lawrence Pickup, auctioneer, at the house of Robert Kitchine, at Hill Brigg within Withnell (Chorley) on Thursday, the 21st day of January, 1796: All sorts of *household goods*, beds and bedding, one good carding engine, a Roving Billy, three Spinning Jennies and one Cow together with a huge quantity of hay. All under 20s. ready money.

Advertisement.

On Sunday morning the 21st inst., a gentleman who had slept the previous night at the Swan Inn in Chorley, having brought his great-coat into the parlour preparatory to setting off for Bolton, a man in the room very deliberately put it on in the presence of several people and decamped therewith. The villain was pursued and apprehended the same day, but through mistaken identity, was suffered to escape that justice which his conduct merited for a small pecuniary consideration for the trouble in pursuing him. Whose life or property can be safe if crimes are thus shamefully compromised?

Blackburn Mail, *31 January 1790.*

Canine sagacity. Mr Brodie, landlord of The Squirrel, in Anderton, having a cow which he wished to dispose of, three men from Bolton called one day last week and bargained for her. In a short time, they left The Squirrel with their purchase and drove her quietly as far as Dufflocker on their way to Bolton. Here, on a sudden, a dog belonging to Mr Brodie, which had followed them, courageously liberated the cow and in spite of the efforts of the three men, drove her quickly to his master's house, much to the surprise of the family and the chagrin of the jobbers, who did not seem to relish this extra journey.

Blackburn Mail, 9 July 1828.

Children's Employment Commission, 1841 – J. L. Kennedy reporting on Lancashire Print Grounds and Miscellaneous Trades:

> Mr Wood, an extensive surgical instrument maker in Manchester, speaking of the frequency of hernia in all ranks of life, states that he believes that one person in every seven either requires a truss or uses one; or certainly one in every ten. I am informed by a competent authority that in the neighbourhood of Bakewell, Ashford and Hassop in Derbyshire, the number is much greater, as high as one in three; and the same authority states that few men arrive at old age in this district without being affected in this manner.
>
> The district being very hilly, and the fences, for the most part, of stone, requiring to be climbed over, are supposed to increase any tendency to hernia. In a list of applicants at Manchester Infirmary for leg supports from July, 1837, to May, 1839, it is curious to observe that of 60 cases, 51 were under nine years of age at the time of making the application, and that of these, 45 cases occurred under four-and-a-half years of age.
>
> Mr Wood: I do not attribute crooked limbs so much to employment at early periods of life as to natural debility, as in by far the greater number of cases it shows itself before the child is of sufficient age to work at all, and in many cases, before it has been put to the ground.

On Tuesday, Binns, the late hangman, pitched his tent behind the New Inn Yard and, with a dummy figure, performed mimic executions during the evening before the eyes of many Haslingden people, whose morbid curiosity had been aroused. Binns also showed relics of certain murderers he had executed.

Rossendale Free Press, 14 April 1888.

The clogger's art:

Around the turn of the century, a clogger would spend about 40 minutes making a pair of soles, and perhaps another two hours completing the clogs, so that if he did all the work himself, he would be able to complete three or four pairs a day.

Soles were sometimes made by journeymen cloggers and in the larger shops, there would be varying degrees of specialisation. The traditional wood for soles is alder, although sycamore was also used. Both are fairly hard, close-grained woods which resist water, and can take nails without splitting.

The village clogger used to buy his wood in the form of clog blocks, made by gypsies and other family groups, who set up temporary camps in the alder groves of Ireland, Scotland, Wales and the North of England.

They felled alders measuring 18 inches to 24 inches in girth and sawed them into logs around 16 inches long. Each log was then cleft along the grain to yield two pieces of wood, each slightly larger than the size of a sole. These were then roughly shaped into clog blocks using a stock knife. The blocks were made while timber was still green after felling, and then they were arranged in open sacks to season before being sold to the clogger. Modern clog soles are made from beech, which is difficult to cut with a stock knife, but which cuts very well by machine. It is harder than alder.

The best clogs were made from *kip*. This is cow hide treated with wax at the tannery and usually stained black on the flesh side. It is very durable, and yet it is supple enough to stretch well over the last. It moulds comfortably to the foot. Cheaper clogs would be made from split kip, but they would not wear as well as best kip. Cardies were even cheaper. These were made from thick, greasy leathers which came off the carding machines in textile mills. The cheapest clogs were 'old tops', made from the uppers of old boots.

In 1900, clog irons were made at forges from square-shaped rods of mild steel. The steel was worked red-hot in all the processes. Later, they were made cold from specially-formed mild steel rods with a channel on one side. The rods were shaped by a rotary machine and holes punched for the nails. Best kip uppers could last 20 years or more if they were well tended, but they would need new soles and many new irons in that time.

The Clog Maker, Colne Valley Museum, Golcar, near Huddersfield.

theatre royal: Chorley had never seen anything like Mark Lorne before. He was tall, and his immaculate evening dress and top hat gave him an air of distinction as he did his stuff in front of the house. Mark Lorne was a go-getter. He introduced the famous Dr Brodie to Chorley. With his electric gadgets, Dr Brodie used to put life into the sick, the lame, and the lazy. His patients went on stage using crutches or leg irons and threw them away as they went off. A popular slogan at the Theatre Royal at the time was, 'Read, Mark, Lorne.'

Newspaper account, 1953, recalling the year 1911.

I was playing the Duchess of York in Richard III when the part of Ena Sharples cropped up in *Coronation Street*. I did not want to know. I was getting out of the Northern scene; not that I despise it – I am fiercely North Country. But I was moving. They could not find anyone to play Ena. I said, 'Don't be ridiculous. I've lived with this woman all my life.' There is one in every street in every town and city in every country in the world. She is always there. She pontificates. She routs those who will not work. She praises those who will. She is there when there is a new baby and she looks after the mother when there is nobody else to do it. She is there if anybody is sick. If they died she would go and lay them out and have the tea ready when they came back from the funeral.

We had one next door to us when I was a little girl. If ever there was anything wrong, she was there. And I said to them: 'Why did you find this thing difficult?' They had twenty-four women for audition and this was ridiculous. She is as plain as the nose on your face. I romped home. It was easy. I was back in my own childhood with the woman next door, and that was it. It trapped me. It made me, if you like. It went all over the world, but it destroyed me, because nobody sees me or anything about me. They introduce me as Ena Sharples at meetings.

Violet Carson, actress.

Liverpool gentlemen, Manchester men, Bolton chaps.

Anon.

Lancashire ... a county that gives itself the airs of a continent. Southport ... where good Lancashire people go before they die.

Haslam Mills, writer.

What has happened to the muck tips in Rochdale? My father had a little hen pen with two cabins, one for hens, the other for people. I discovered later he had people betting there. It was his little Monte Carlo. He would work very hard, make a lot of money, then get a cab and stay in it until the money was gone – going round and round, singing at the top of his voice.

Gracie Fields, talking to me at her home in Capri.

I remember my father, a market trader, ordering tulips from Amsterdam, and they arrived on Blackburn market at 4 p.m. on a Saturday, a disastrous time. Furthermore, the petals were dropping off. I cried. I saw the whole family business vanishing. There were these grotesque blotches of tulips with black stamens or whatever. Father got a card and wrote, 'Fresh in from Amsterdam, the parrot tulip. New breed.' We did not sell all of them, but we made a big dent in the disaster.

Russell Harty, broadcaster.

I lived in a period which could not be imagined today, of poverty when we had all sorts of problems. You might have a good week,

and a week when the main meal was pobs – bread cut into cubes with tea and condensed milk poured over it. People seemed to get on very well. We were not ill. You never used to hear the word frustration. You never heard the word complex. If you had a sore throat, my old grandmother used to say, 'Put some brown paper on your chest.' And if you had this or that you put a hot water bottle against your stomach. What I think is missing now is the spirit of individual risk. Although the Welfare State has been a godsend to people who need it, we pay a price.

Sir Neville Cardus.

21

THE YEARS OF TUMULT

THE AMERICAN CIVIL WAR broke out in April 1861, with disastrous effect upon the cotton trade. In October 1861 mills began to run short-time, or to close, and there were 3,000 additional applicants for poor relief in the 28 Poor Law Unions. In November, there was an increase of 7,000 and another increase of 7,000 in December. In January 1862 another 16,000 applied for relief, and in February 9,000 more. By July the distress increased like a flood. In August, the flood had become a deluge, 'at which the stoutest heart might stand appalled.'

Before the end of the year the applicants for relief were increasing by thousands a day. As winter approached, the authorities were at their wits' end for the wherewithal to supply hundreds of thousands in want of food, much of the clothing and other necessaries having been pledged or sold to procure food, and from 25 to 47 per cent of the population of the whole manufacturing districts were receiving relief.

It is estimated that more than 420,000 persons were engaged in the cotton trade at that time, every one of whom was affected by the shortage of cotton, but of course, it affected all the other trades and businesses. Shopkeepers were ruined in every town and village. The country rose in sympathy and large amounts were raised in record time for the assistance of the sufferers.

The Mansion House Fund exceeded half a million pounds. A committee of the Lancashire noblemen and Members of Parliament raised £52,000. Mr Cobden, in an appeal, stated that the loss in wages alone was at the rate of £136,094 a week.

Accrington Chronology and Men of Mark.

I wish we had some of the spirit of former times back in the country. *King Cotton* (450,000 words) took me five years to write. I dedicated it to the people of Lancashire and there was a joke about it at the time because I am a Yorkshireman. If ever there were heroes, it was the Lancastrians. Any time during the American Civil War, they could have had the cotton coming over here, and they would not. They starved. And it has never been particularly well known, this fact. They are very different from Yorkshire people, you know, more laughing, more generous. Lancashire has had some terrible times, some shocking times, but it always produced very funny characters; like one I remember who used to invite all the show girls to dinner in Manchester and have the staff of one of the big hotels lined up by the hall porter so that he could put a £5 note in every hand.

Thomas Armstrong, author of various works, including Master of Bankdam, *talking to me at his Dales home in Gunnerside.*

1842: Mobs went from mill to mill and from town to town in East Lancashire knocking boiler plugs out, thus forcibly stopping the machinery, the Chartists having resolved that all work should cease until the government yielded the Six Points of the Charter. These were: universal suffrage; vote by ballot; annual parliaments; no property qualification; payment of representatives; and division of the country into parliamentary districts.

> This part of the country is in a deplorable state, for hundreds and thousands have neither work nor meat. They are daily begging in the streets of Haslingden, 20 or 30 together crying for bread; meetings are held every Sunday on the neighbouring hills, attended by thousands of poor, hungry, haggard people wishing for any change, even though it should be death. On Sunday last, a meeting was held on the hills near Accrington [Whinney Hill] and the persons present, it is said, covered an area of 4,420 square yards of ground. The speakers were in a wagon in the centre and there must have been 26,000 present. The speakers, ten in number, were very violent, advising their hearers never to petition Parliament again, but to be determined to have a redress of grievances immediately. The people ... say they might as well die by the sword as by hunger.
>
> *From a Liverpool newspaper.*

On Saturday, the 13th, the mob entered Accrington from Haslingden, attacking R. and M. Smith's printworks at Baxenden, which they stopped by letting the steam and water out of the boiler; then on to Hargreaves and Dugdale's at Broad Oak, and Denham and Grimshaw's. At Messrs Hargreaves's cotton mills, where about 1,000 are employed, after emptying the boiler, they let off the reservoir; then on to Christy's foundry and Cunliffe's engraving shop where, after letting off the boiler, they turned out all the hands.

One man said that if the workpeople went into Hargreaves's again they would return and set it on fire. From Accrington, they went to Clayton, where they stopped the soapworks, as well as the mills. Then on to Fort and Company's Printworks at Church. On the Monday following, 3,000 to 4,000 of a mob from Haslingden and Bury proceeded to Blackburn, and damaged and stopped several mills. A company of the 72nd Highlanders intercepted the rioters and took 18 prisoners, and a further lot of 14 were taken at James Eccles's Mill. The mob threw stones at the military as they drove off with their prisoners, and the military then fired upon the crowd, wounding five or six persons, including a woman who had taken no part in the riot.

From the Manchester Guardian, *17 August 1842.*

1826 – Power loom riots: Trade was bad, prices of provisions very high, and the cause of distress was blamed on power looms. Serious riots broke out in Accrington, Haslingden, Clitheroe, Darwen, Chorley, Bolton, Manchester, etc., and at Chadderton, special constables were sworn in and the military called out, a number of men being arrested. Ten of them (seven men and three women) were transported for life, four men were sentenced to 18 months' imprisonment, seven others to 12 months' imprisonment, ten men and one woman to six months, seven men and three women for three months. Compensations were granted to many people who had suffered in East Lancashire.

Accrington Chronology and Men of Mark.

Blackburn, with its teeming population, is at the present time behind every other town in England in intelligence, for it appears that out of every 100 men only 39 can write their own names, and out of 100 women, only 11 are able to do so, while in London, 89 men and 76 women out of every 100 are able to read and write.

Directors of the town's Mechanics' Institution, March 1844.

> All is filthiness without me; all is ignorance within;
> I ache with cramps, I shake with damps,
> Oh! the warmth of glorious gin.

Quoted by P. A. Whittle, Blackburn As It Is *(1852).*

> High in the belfry the old Sexton stands,
> Grasping the rope with his thin, bony hands;
> Fixed is his gaze as by some magic spell,
> Till he hears the distant murmur, Ring, Ring the Bell!

From Chorley Union Year Book: Workhouse officers' dietary table, fixed by resolution of the Board of Guardians, 20 March 1906:

Per week – 6lbs. flour, 4lbs. meat and quarter-pound suet, three-quarters pound butter, 1lb. lump sugar, three-quarters pound raw sugar, 4oz. tea, 4oz. coffee or cocoa, or 3oz. tea in lieu, half pound cheese or sixpennyworth fruit, 1lb. bacon, or half-pound bacon and quarter-pound butter extra, half pound lard, eight-and-a-half pints milk, half-pound preserves or marmalade, 7lbs. potatoes, four eggs, sixpennyworth fish, 4oz. rice or tapioca or sago or semolina, vegetables as required, half-pound currants or raisins, plus vinegar, salt, pepper, mustard and yeast as required.

Tasks of work, casual paupers who remain for one night only:

As regards MALES – The breaking of two cwt. of stones or such other quantity not less than one-and-a-half cwt. nor more than four cwt., as the Guardians, having regard to the nature of the stone, may prescribe. The stone shall be broken to such a size as the Guardians, having regard to the nature of the stone, may prescribe; or the picking of one pound of unbeaten, or two pounds of beaten, oakum, or three hours' work in digging, or pumping, or cutting wood or grinding corn.

As regards FEMALES – The picking of half a pound of unbeaten, or one pound of beaten, oakum, or three hours' work in washing, or scrubbing and cleaning.

Casual paupers who are detained for more than one night:

As regards MALES, for each entire day of detention – The breaking of seven cwt. of stone, or such other quantity not less than five cwt., nor more than 13 cwt., as the Guardians, having regard to the nature of the stone, may prescribe. The stone shall be broken to such a size as the Guardians, having regard to the nature thereof, may prescribe; or the picking of four pounds of unbeaten, or eight pounds of beaten, oakum; or nine hours' work in digging, or pumping, or cutting wood, or grinding corn.

As regards FEMALES, for each entire day of detention – The picking of two pounds of unbeaten, or four pounds of beaten, oakum; or nine hours' work in washing, scrubbing, cleaning, or needlework.

James and William Greenwood, aged eight and six, of Carrs, Haslingden, died through excessive bathing.

Accrington Observer, 1919.

I can remember Owd Totty, Owd Boiler, Owd Legs and particularly
Owd Dick Soot, whose wife, Mrs Swarbrick, when asked if a Mr
Swarbrick lived at her home, said she had never heard of him. I
could take you to a village shop where the musical son of a musical
father is proud of the Christian name of Verdi, painted above his
door. This has a precedent in a character named Robert Bannister,
of Barrowford, a brass band enthusiast who, it is recorded, had seven
sons: Handel Orridge, Haydn Novello, Julian Mozart, Mendelssohn

Shelton, Robert Rossini, Beethoven Reeves Best Park and Irvine Verdi William Tell.

> *Sylvia Corbridge, It's An Old Lancashire Custom, quoted in*
> Journal of Lancashire Dialect Society, *12, January 1963.*

You're like everybody else – you think we all walk about in cloth caps looking bloody gormless, every house with a euphonium in the wardrobe and a whippet in the scullery.

> *Vic in Stan Barstow's The Watcher on the Shore.*

A weaver's work on ordinary looms, average times:

> Replenish shuttle (skewering cop) 11 seconds, repairing warp breaks 45 seconds, repairing weft breaks 20 seconds, finding pick two minutes, removing cloth (per cut 80 yards) five minutes, cleaning/picking cloth (per cut) up to half an hour, fetching weft (say) 15 minutes per day, oiling and sweeping (say), 30 minutes per week.

One can not help but be critical to the extent that nobody could have had such opportunities as the textile people had in Lancashire from 1945 to 1951. Companies later losing money doing the same volume or more were making a million pounds a year then. What has happened to the money? How much of it was spent in re-equipment? Almost all the people you speak to say it is the government, and they will also say to you that they really had no long-term confidence in textiles. It is easy for them to blame the government. It is easy for somebody to say, well, I did not pass my exams; I had a bad master. Why is it that I can go into the textile trade and be successful? I have not found anyone in Lancashire who likes anyone else in Lancashire.

> *Joe Hyman, industrialist, talking to me when he was head of Viyella.*

WELL-DRESSED FOR 50s.: Tacklers, like other citizens, must wear clothes, and there is no reason why they should not be smart, well-cut garments of good quality. Suits in strong, hard-wearing tweed, made to measure in the CWS factories by Trade Union labour, can be had from 50s. A smart blue serge suit, guaranteed not to fade, from 84s.

> *Advertisement c. 1924.*

Wigan ... I became surrounded by cottages, old cottages. Heads and shoulders peered over walls and stared long and fixedly at me. Witty remarks were bandied from neighbour to neighbour over rickety garden fences, and an extraordinary old man, without a hair on his head, and with no teeth, stumbled out of a cottage and mumbled a flood of unintelligible remarks within two inches of my face. And from these cottages I came to more, and to trams, and to high walls about large mills, with tall chimneys, rising to the sky, and clumsy, fantastic, and complicated erections with mysterious functions. All the ground was packed with buildings of strictly practical designs and set at odd, incomprehensible angles, and it was surprising how few people were about. I walked alone among all this human achievement until I was astounded to see two men squatting on the kerb at one of the corners.

They squatted calmly, like Indian fakirs, but why on the kerbstone, which was only an inch high, did not seem very clear. They seemed very small and very odd, with nothing to lean their backs against, and stuck out there on a corner, down on the ground, in the hunched-up squat, I nodded and mumbled a 'how do?' But the searching expression of the two faces was fixed, and as I passed, the four eyes moved slowly across their sockets from left to right. There was no change of expression and no acknowledgement, either in amity or mockery.

Walter Wilkinson, an itinerant entertainer,
Puppets through Lancashire *(1936)*.

22

WHERE STAND WE NOW?

ORTH VERSUS SOUTH seemed much too simple an antithesis, even if anybody had ever taken the trouble to decide where exactly the Midlands came into it. Yet all over the North, I came across instances of the powerful animus which the South or Southern attitudes provoked. There was the man from Batley who pictured the North as a fat and generous sow lying on her side while the greedy little piglets (the South) fed off her. There were novelists like Stan Barstow and Sid Chaplin who told me how much they resented constantly being asked *why* they chose to live in the North, as if they were displaying some deplorable eccentricity.

There were the civic dignitaries in the North-East who exploded with passion against the Establishment and all its works, and who told me that there would be a 'bloody uprising' if 'they' again left the area helpless under the impact of another slump ... Here, plainly, were two separate worlds, two different philosophies of life. This was a place beyond the London–Birmingham axis of prosperity, a place with a keen sense of its own identity and its own unique heritage; a place, too, where the hurts of history still had a sting in them.

Graham Turner, The North Country, published in the late 'sixties.

Like the poor, this North–South divide is always with us. Once, I could write about it with passion. Now I can hardly write about it at all. Once, the issue was clear-cut. Now, all is confused. This is what I wrote many years ago:

Almost unnoticed, British Rail has bridged the gap between North and South, speeding whole regiments of both clans in daily inter-course, reducing the need for missionaries in the wastelands above Birmingham, and allowing the fortress towns to reduce their defences and neglect their outer walls.

So busy is the line between London and the North that some commuters swear the trains do not actually move, but are permanently positioned, one end in Manchester, the other at Euston, and vast numbers of people walk the whole distance along its corridors.

The point is: do we Northerners measure up? Or do we, secretly, still consider that any Southerner approaching our hen pens is a marauder, fair game for the stewpot, or both?

If you have in your pantry courgettes, saffron, chilli powder, olive oil, yogurt, cloves, black peppercorns, sauerkraut or garlic, you are Southern and therefore THEM.

Pickled red cabbage, Daddies Sauce, lemon in plastic lemon, English mustard (rather than German or Dijon), ready-ground pepper, potato cakes, cooking fat – US.

Easy chairs in black leather, tiny prints in heavy frames, wooden kitchen utensils, TV either ancient ten-inch or filling half a wall with colour – THEM.

Matching three-piece, lace curtains, ashtrays labelled 'A present from – ', clocks with gilt, get off me foot, lawns with flower borders, daffs in plant pots (rather than rubber plants) – US.

Salami in bundles, strings of onions pinned to kitchen walls, steady on, old chap, French butter, wine for cooking, heavy cast-iron pans from France – THEM.

Toilets, closets – US.

Lavatories, loos, johns – THEM.

Books – US.

Book reviews – THEM.

Leftover duck salad with bottle of Beaune for supper – THEM.

Egg and chips, pokers, bottom drawers, hairnets, red lipstick, union shirts, woollen underwear, pint bottles of pale ale, braces, short back and sides, fine weather for ducks, big letter headings marked 'Estimates free', cars costing £850 – US.

Dichotomy, pragmatic, soupçon, actually, Ciao!, four-letter words in mixed company – THEM.

Where's my shirt?, bleached hair, jeans, wrong Tube trains, going for a pint, Talk of the Town – US visiting THEM.

Bowlers on back of head – US, if we are rent collectors, bookies or taxi proprietors; THEM if they are drunk.

'Come on me old darling,' 'Look, lovely,' 'Hi, sweetie!', window boxes, plain drinking glasses with heavy bases, Vichy water, old girl – THEM (and they refer to the Barnet by-pass as the start of the North).

'Going out tonight' – meaning a farce, Jimmy Tarbuck or *Cinderella on Ice* followed by a Cornish pasty and a bunch of fives up the hooter – US (as are port and lemon, Babycham, grey flannel trousers, turnups, shoe laces).

'Going out tonight' – meaning a couple of gins, Japanese movie, cannelloni by candle-light with the wrong woman, bistro, chianti from raffia bottles – THEM.

Brown paint, cream and green, I've supped some ale, flowered bedspreads, thistles, nettles, pit shaft, hen pen, payment in cash, allotment – US.

Creepers, yellow, orange or architect-green paint, books on antiques, four-tone car horn, pub named Barley Mow – THEM.

Groups of twenty paddling in Trafalgar Square with Nelson – US.

Groups of twenty swimming the Serpentine – THEM.

Having said all this, if one inspects, carefully, the constituent parts of THEM, one finds that, ten years ago, they were all US, and have migrated.

The fact that they have flowered ties, polished insteps, slender briefcases, worry beads, mohair suits and Chihuahuas named Fidel need not confuse you.

Next year, given a good following wind, it could be you.

I find, looking back on that summary, that the North has, indeed, adopted many of the Southern preferences. Any one of the foods and condiments I ascribed to them are in my larder.

Have the distinctions blurred?

I rather think they have. I was once convinced that as Northerners went South they hid their origins and felt a deep sense of unease and lack of confidence. When Russell Harty, that Blackburnian abroad, lay dying, he made some reference to Princess Margaret asking about him, 'twice', a sure indication that he was suffering from the insecurity of a lifetime.

But there is no general rule to be observed and it would be wrong to seek one. Alan Bennett remains unruffled by his Southern adoption. He has not altered his accent or his habits one jot so far as I can see. The same might be said of a fellow Yorkshireman, David Hockney, and of those various pop and rock stars who (like Cilla Black) headed South for a lorra lolly. Maureen Lipman is gloriously Maureen Lipman; and one could add to the list endlessly.

It is the anonymous people who hide their origins most: the minor civil servants, and company men; salesmen, white youths with moustaches driving Sierras and calling themselves middle-management.

So I would rather not join in this old argument at this stage of my life because I am easy about drinking in Barnsley or Barnstaple. Any sense of unease long ago left me. Perhaps Dijon mustard has had an effect on me.

One or two accusations do hold good, however.

The South is insular. Its senior civil servants know Brussels rather better than they know Leeds. Too much money has been invested in the South-East to the detriment of the rest of us.

I might quote Edward Heath on this: 'Whitehall exists between Watford and Haywards Heath.'

Or Lord James of Rusholme: 'It is twice as far from London to Harrogate as it is from Harrogate to London.'

Sadly true.

Beyond that, I think it is time we stopped looking over our shoulders at the South and got on with our own business.

It took the Japanese to show what could be done with a car industry in the North-East.

Why couldn't we do that?